CASSEROLE COOKING

Edited by
Hilary Walden

octopus

CONTENTS

This edition first published 1978 by
Octopus Books Limited
59 Grosvenor Street, London W.1.

© 1978 Octopus Books Limited

ISBN 0 7064 0696 6

Produced and printed in Hong Kong by
Mandarin Publishers Limited
22a Westlands Road, Quarry Bay

Frontispiece: TURKEY WITH LEMON AND CAPERS *(page 68) (Photograph:
British Turkey Federation)*

Weights and Measures

All measurements in this book are based on Imperial weights and measures, with American equivalents given in parenthesis.

Measurements in *weight* in the Imperial and American system are the same. Measurements in *volume* are different, and the following table shows the equivalents:

Spoon measurements

Imperial	U.S.
1 tablespoon	1 tablespoon
1½ tablespoons	2 tablespoons
2 tablespoons	3 tablespoons
	(abbrev: T)

Level spoon measurements are used in all the recipes.

Liquid measurements

1 Imperial pint	20 fluid ounces
1 American pint	16 fluid ounces
1 American cup	8 fluid ounces

INTRODUCTION

The term 'casserole' is used to describe those dishes in which the main ingredient is cooked in a liquid or sauce in a closed container. Usually a casserole is cooked in the dish in which it is served. The main ingredient can be meat, poultry, game, fish, vegetables or even fruit. Additional vegetables, herbs, spices and seasonings are cooked with the main ingredient to impart flavour. The liquid may be stock, wine, fruit or vegetable juice, cider or beer.

Casserole cooking is perhaps the most convenient and simplest of all cooking methods. Most casseroles require little attention during cooking so you can pop the meal in the oven and forget about it for an hour or more. Casseroles can be assembled in advance. This is an advantage for those at work who have to rely on an automatic oven timer or another member of the family to start cooking the main meal.

Casseroles will not spoil if they are not served the minute they are cooked so if the family or guests arrive late, dinner won't be ruined. Another advantage is the time saved washing up since most casseroles require the use of only one or two pans.

There is a vast selection of casserole cookware available in the shops today. Attractive oven-to-tableware is produced in a wide range of materials but for ease of preparation it is worth investing in a flameproof casserole.

Flameproof casseroles can be used over direct heat on top of the cooker and in the oven. The same pot can thus be used for initial frying, cooking in the oven and serving at the table.

Part of the secret of a good casserole lies in the careful addition of flavouring herbs and spices. Although specific flavourings are suggested in these recipes don't be afraid to experiment. There are no hard and fast rules concerning which herbs or spices go with particular foods. The amount of seasoning, herbs or spices to be added is largely a matter of personal taste but these flavourings should never be added in such quantities that they mask the taste of the main ingredients.

Some of the recipes suggest fresh herbs. If these are unobtainable, substitute the dried equivalent but be sure to use only one third of the recommended fresh quantity because dried herbs have a much stronger flavour.

A successful casserole depends on long slow cooking. This is particularly true when using cheaper cuts of meat. Although the recipes in this book have been written for oven cooking, most are suitable for cooking on top of the cooker in a flameproof casserole or heavy-based saucepan. The only proviso is a very gentle heat and occasional stirring. It's worth remembering 'a stew boiled is a stew spoiled'.

Meat, poultry and game casseroles are ideal cooked dishes for freezing. It takes little extra effort to prepare double quantities and freeze half, providing a source of ready cooked meals in the freezer.

Casseroles should be cooled then frozen in rigid foil, polythene or waxed containers. Alternatively line the casserole dish with foil and add the cooked food. Cool thoroughly then freeze until firm. Take the food in the foil lining out of the casserole, wrap and seal in a polythene bag. Return to the freezer.

Herbs, strong spices and aromatics, such as garlic and chives, continue to develop flavours in the freezer so it is preferable to add these after thawing before reheating. It is also wise to omit potatoes from casseroles to be frozen because these tend to lose texture. Simply add parboiled potatoes before reheating, if required. Cream should only be added to casseroles after freezing and thawing.

Ideally, casseroles should be thawed completely before reheating. If there isn't sufficient time for thawing at room temperature, return the frozen food to the casserole and heat in a moderate oven, 350°F, Gas Mark 4 for 1-1½ hours depending on the size of the casserole.

8   BEEF AND MUSHROOM LAYER CASSEROLE *(page 10) (Photograph: M.E.A.T.)*

BEEF CASSEROLES

Beef and Mushroom Layer Casserole

3 tablespoons (¼ cup) oil
2 lb. braising steak, cut into 6 slices
3 onions, sliced
8 oz. (2 cups) mushrooms, sliced
1 red pepper, cored, seeded and sliced
1 teaspoon salt

freshly ground black pepper
½ teaspoon dried tarragon
1 tablespoon chopped fresh parsley
1 tablespoon tomato purée
¼ pint (⅔ cup) beef stock (bouillon)

Heat the oil in a frying pan over moderate heat. Brown each slice of meat for 2-3 minutes on each side. Remove from the pan and keep warm. Lower the heat and fry the onions gently for 5 minutes until soft but not browned. Add the mushrooms, red pepper, salt, pepper and herbs and fry for a further 2-3 minutes. Stir in the tomato purée and stock and bring to the boil, stirring.

Spoon a little of the vegetable mixture into the base of a deep casserole, then arrange a layer of meat on top. Continue these layers finishing with a layer of vegetables. Cover and cook in a moderate oven, 350°F, Gas Mark 4 for 45 minutes until the meat is tender.

Taste and adjust the seasoning if necessary. Serve each portion of meat topped with the mushroom mixture.

Serves 6

Beef Casserole with Noodles

1 oz. (¼ cup) flour
1 teaspoon salt
freshly ground black pepper
1½ lb. braising steak, cut into 1
  inch cubes
3 tablespoons (¼ cup) oil
2 onions, sliced
2 sticks celery, sliced
15 oz. can tomatoes
1 tablespoon tomato purée

¼ pint (⅔ cup) beef stock
  (bouillon) or wine
8 oz. (2 cups) mushrooms, sliced
1 teaspoon chopped fresh
  marjoram
1 teaspoon chopped fresh
  rosemary
4 oz. (1 cup) noodles
4 oz. (1 cup) Cheddar cheese,
  grated

Combine the flour with the salt and pepper. Toss the meat in the seasoned flour to coat well. Heat the oil in a flameproof casserole over moderate heat and add the beef. Fry briskly until evenly browned. Remove. Lower the heat and add the onions and celery to the casserole. Fry gently for 5 minutes, stirring occasionally, until soft but not browned.

Return the meat to the casserole and add the tomatoes, tomato purée, stock or wine, mushrooms and herbs. Bring to the boil. Cover and cook in a moderate oven, 350°F, Gas Mark 4 for 2 hours.

Fifteen minutes before the end of the cooking time, cook the noodles in boiling salted water until just tender. Drain thoroughly then add to the casserole. Taste and adjust the seasoning, if necessary. Sprinkle with the grated cheese and place under a hot grill for about 5 minutes until the cheese is melted and golden.

Serves 4

Beef Carbonnade

3 tablespoons (¼ cup) oil
1 large onion, finely chopped
2 lb. braising steak, cut into 1 inch
  cubes
¾ pint (2 cups) light ale
2 teaspoons French mustard
2 teaspoons brown sugar

2 teaspoons malt vinegar
1 bay leaf
1 teaspoon dried thyme
1 teaspoon salt
freshly ground black pepper
2 oz. (1 cup) fresh breadcrumbs

Heat the oil in a flameproof casserole over moderate heat. Add the onion and fry gently for 5 minutes until soft and translucent. Add the beef and fry for 5 minutes, turning frequently, until browned on all sides.

Stir in the ale, mustard, sugar, vinegar, herbs, salt and pepper. Bring to the boil, continuing to stir. Cover and cook in a moderate oven, 350°F, Gas Mark 4 for 2 hours or until the beef is tender.

Remove from the oven and stir in the breadcrumbs. Taste and adjust the seasoning and remove the bay leaf before serving.

Serves 6

Peppered Beef

1 oz. (¼ cup) flour
salt
freshly ground black pepper
½ teaspoon ground ginger
2 lb. top (standing) rib of beef
4 tablespoons (⅓ cup) oil
1 large carrot, peeled and sliced
Sauce:
¼ teaspoon Tabasco sauce
¼ pint (⅔ cup) dry red wine
8 oz. can tomatoes

4 oz. (1 cup) button mushrooms,
  sliced
2 tablespoons (3T) brown sugar
2 tablespoons (3T) white wine
  vinegar
2 garlic cloves, crushed
1 bay leaf
1 green pepper, cored, seeded
  and sliced
1 red pepper, cored, seeded and
  sliced

In a bowl or large polythene bag combine the flour, salt, pepper and ginger. Add the meat and toss to coat well. Shake to remove excess flour.

Heat the oil in a large pan, fry the beef quickly until evenly browned. Transfer to a casserole dish. Fry the carrot in the oil remaining in the pan for 2 minutes. Place in the casserole.

Heat all the sauce ingredients, except the peppers, in the saucepan, stirring. When the sauce is boiling, pour over the meat. Cover the casserole and place in a moderate oven, 325°F, Gas Mark 3 for 1½ hours.

Add the peppers to the casserole and continue to cook, covered, for 30 minutes. Taste and adjust the seasoning, if necessary. Remove the bay leaf before serving.
Serves 4-6

Beef Braised in Soy Sauce

½ pint (1¼ cups) water
3 tablespoons (¼ cup) soy sauce
5 tablespoons (6T) dry sherry
2½ teaspoons castor (superfine)
  sugar

salt and pepper
2½ tablespoons (3T) vegetable oil
2 lb. lean stewing beef, cut into 1
  inch cubes

Combine the water, soy sauce, sherry, sugar, salt and pepper in a bowl.

Heat 1½ tablespoons (2T) of the oil in a heavy frying pan almost to smoking point. Add just enough meat to cover the base of the pan and fry quickly for 2 minutes or until lightly browned on all sides. Brown the rest of the meat, adding the remaining oil as necessary.

Transfer the meat to a casserole. Pour the soy sauce mixture into the pan and bring to the boil. Pour over the meat, cover and place the casserole in a moderate oven, 350°F, Gas Mark 4. Cook for 1½-2 hours or until the meat is tender.
Serves 4-6

PEPPERED BEEF *(Photograph: M.E.A.T.)*

Steak and Mushroom Casserole

3 tablespoons (¼ cup) oil
1 ½ lb. braising steak, cut into 2
  inch cubes
4 small onions, quartered
8 oz. (2 cups) mushrooms, sliced
salt and pepper
1 teaspoon dry mustard
1 tablespoon chopped fresh
  parsley

2 tablespoons (3T) tomato purée
½ pint (1 ¼ cups) beef stock
  (bouillon)
1 tablespoon cornflour
  (cornstarch)
1 tablespoon water
2 tomatoes, peeled, seeded and
  cut into strips

Heat the oil in a flameproof casserole over moderate heat. Add the meat
and fry for 5-7 minutes, stirring frequently, until evenly browned. Remove
the meat with a slotted spoon. Add the onions and mushrooms to the
casserole and fry over gentle heat for 3-4 minutes until softened but not
browned, stirring occasionally.

Add the salt, pepper, dry mustard, chopped parsley, tomato purée and
the stock and bring to the boil. Replace the meat in the casserole. Cover
and cook in a moderate oven, 350°F, Gas Mark 4 for 2 hours.

Blend the cornflour with the water. Stir into the casserole and bring to
the boil on top of the cooker, stirring constantly. Taste and adjust the
seasoning, if necessary. Serve garnished with strips of tomato.
Serves 4

Beef and Apple Casserole

1 oz. (¼ cup) flour
1 teaspoon dry mustard
salt and pepper
1 ½ lb. stewing steak, cut into 2
  inch cubes
2 oz. (¼ cup) beef dripping
2 onions, sliced
2 carrots, peeled and sliced

2 tablespoons (3T) malt vinegar
4 oz. (1 cup) mushrooms, sliced
1 tablespoon grated lemon rind
1 teaspoon dried mixed herbs
¾ pint (2 cups) beef stock
  (bouillon)
1 large cooking apple, peeled,
  cored and thinly sliced

Combine the flour with mustard, salt and pepper. Toss the meat in the
seasoned flour. Heat the fat in a flameproof casserole over a moderate
heat. Add the meat and fry briskly, turning frequently, until evenly
browned. Take out the meat and set aside. Add the onions and carrots to
the casserole and fry for 3-4 minutes until golden brown. Remove.

Add the vinegar to the remaining fat and boil until it has reduced by
about half. Return the meat and fried vegetables to the casserole and add
the mushrooms, lemon rind, herbs and stock. Bring to the boil, stirring.

Cover and cook in a moderate oven, 325°F, Gas Mark 3 for 2 hours.
Add the apple and continue to cook, covered, for 30 minutes. Taste and
adjust the seasoning, if necessary, before serving.
Serves 4

Boeuf Bourguignon

3 tablespoons (¼ cup) oil
3 lb. lean stewing beef, cut into 1½
  inch cubes
6 oz. streaky (fatty) bacon,
  derinded and diced
1 carrot, peeled and sliced
1 onion, sliced
1 teaspoon salt
freshly ground black pepper
2 oz. (½ cup) flour
¾ pint (2 cups) beef stock
  (bouillon)
¾ pint (2 cups) Burgundy or other
  red wine

1 tablespoon tomato purée
2 garlic cloves, crushed
1 teaspoon chopped fresh or ⅓
  teaspoon dried thyme
1 bay leaf
2 tablespoons (3T) chopped fresh
  parsley
18 button onions
1 lb. button mushrooms
2 oz. (¼ cup) butter
Garnish:
1 tablespoon chopped fresh
  parsley

Heat the oil in a large flameproof casserole, add the beef and fry, stirring, until evenly browned. Remove with a slotted spoon.

Lower the heat and sauté the bacon gently. Remove. Add the carrot and onion to the casserole and cook for 5 minutes over a moderate heat. Return the beef and bacon to the casserole and sprinkle in the salt, pepper and flour, tossing the meat and vegetables to coat thoroughly. Cook for 4 minutes, stirring frequently.

Stir in the stock, wine, tomato purée, garlic and herbs. Bring to the boil. Cover the casserole and place in a moderate oven, 325°F, Gas Mark 3. Cook for 2 hours.

Meanwhile sauté the button onions and mushrooms in the butter over moderate heat for 5 minutes until evenly browned. Add the onions and mushrooms to the casserole, cover and continue cooking for a further 1 hour. Taste and adjust the seasoning, if necessary. Skim off any fat from the surface. Sprinkle with chopped parsley to garnish.
Serves 6-8

Braised Steaks

2 tablespoons (3T) oil
12 oz. braising steak, cut into 2
  slices
1 small onion, chopped
1 carrot, peeled and sliced
1 small swede, peeled and sliced
½ pint (1 ¼ cups) beef stock
  (bouillon)

½ teaspoon salt
freshly ground black pepper
1 tablespoon Worcestershire
  sauce
1 teaspoon dry mustard
½ teaspoon dried mixed herbs

Heat the oil in a flameproof casserole over moderate heat. Fry the meat for 4 minutes on each side until well browned. Remove. Lower the heat and fry the vegetables for 4 minutes until lightly browned, stirring occasionally.

Place the meat on top of the vegetables and pour over sufficient stock just to cover the vegetables, but not the meat. Sprinkle the remaining ingredients onto the stock. Bring to the boil.

Cover and cook in a moderate oven, 350°F, Gas Mark 4 for 1½ hours until the meat is tender. Taste and adjust the seasoning, if necessary. Serve with creamed potatoes.

Serves 2

French Beef Stew

2 oz. (¼ cup) dripping or lard
  (shortening)
2 lb. braising steak, cut into 2 inch
  cubes
1 tablespoon flour
¼ pint (⅔ cup) dry red wine
¼ pint (⅔ cup) beef stock
  (bouillon)

2 cloves garlic, crushed
2 tablespoons (3T) tomato purée
salt
freshly ground black pepper
6 slices streaky (fatty) bacon,
  derinded
20 button onions or shallots
4 oz. (1 cup) button mushrooms

Heat 1½ oz. (3T) dripping or lard in a flameproof casserole over gentle heat. Add the meat, increase the heat to moderate and fry for 5 minutes until well browned on all sides.

Lower the heat and sprinkle in the flour. Cook, stirring, until the flour is lightly browned. Stir in the wine, stock, garlic, tomato purée, salt and pepper. Bring to the boil, stirring constantly. Remove from the heat.

In a frying pan, melt the remaining dripping or lard over moderate heat. Cut the bacon into strips and fry for 3 minutes. Lower the heat, add the onions and fry gently for 5 minutes, turning occasionally until evenly browned. Add the onions and bacon to the meat. Cover the casserole and cook in a moderate oven, 350°F, Gas Mark 4 for 2 hours.

Add the mushrooms and continue to cook, uncovered, for 10-15 minutes. Taste and adjust the seasoning if necessary before serving.

Serves 6

BRAISED STEAKS *(Photograph: M.E.A.T.)*

Beef and Bean Casserole

1 lb. (2 cups) haricot (navy) beans
2½ pints (6¼ cups) water
1½ teaspoons salt
freshly ground black pepper
1 tablespoon oil
1 lb. pork sausages, cut into 1 inch
  slices
2 large onions, finely chopped
2 garlic cloves, crushed (optional)

2 lb. stewing beef, cut into 1 inch
  cubes
½ teaspoon dried savory
1 bay leaf
¼ teaspoon dried marjoram
4 large tomatoes, blanched,
  peeled and sliced
¼ pint (⅔ cup) beef stock
  (bouillon)

Put the beans in a large bowl and cover with cold water. Leave to soak overnight.

Drain and put the beans in a large saucepan. Add the water, 1 teaspoon salt and ½ teaspoon black pepper. Bring to the boil, then reduce the heat and simmer for 1½ hours or until tender. Drain, reserving ¾ pint (2 cups) of the cooking liquor.

Heat the oil in a large pan over moderate heat. Fry the sausage slices for about 10 minutes or until evenly browned. Drain on kitchen paper. Pour off all but 3 tablespoons (¼ cup) of the fat.

Add the chopped onions and garlic, if used, to the pan. Fry, stirring occasionally, until the onions are soft but not brown. Remove the vegetables from the pan and set aside. Raise the heat. Add the beef and more fat, if necessary, and brown the meat quickly on all sides.

Transfer the meat to a large casserole. Stir in the onions, garlic, herbs, ½ teaspoon salt, pepper, tomatoes and stock. Cover the casserole and cook in a cool oven, 300°F, Gas Mark 2 for 2 hours.

Add the beans, the reserved cooking liquor and the sausage slices. Continue cooking for a further 30 minutes to 1 hour or until the beef is tender. Remove the bay leaf before serving.

Serves 6-8

Daube de Boeuf

2 tablespoons (3T) flour
1 teaspoon salt
¼ teaspoon freshly ground black
  pepper
1 teaspoon paprika
2 lb. braising steak, cut into 2 inch
  cubes
4 tablespoons (⅓ cup) oil
4 oz. smoked streaky (fatty)
  bacon, derinded and cut into ½
  inch cubes
1 onion, diced
1 teaspoon chopped fresh thyme
1 teaspoon chopped fresh
  rosemary

2 teaspoons chopped fresh
  parsley
½ pint (1¼ cups) red wine
½ pint (1¼ cups) beef stock
  (bouillon)
8 oz. tomatoes, peeled and
  quartered
3 oz. black (ripe) olives, stoned
4 anchovy fillets, mashed
Garnish:
1 tablespoon chopped fresh
  parsley

Mix the flour, salt, pepper and paprika together, then toss the beef in the seasoned flour to coat evenly.

Heat the oil in a flameproof casserole over moderate heat. Add the beef and fry, stirring, until browned all over. Remove the meat with a slotted spoon and keep warm.

Lower the heat and fry the bacon gently for 2-3 minutes. Add the onion and fry, stirring frequently, for 5 minutes until translucent. Sprinkle in the herbs and add the meat. Stir in the wine and stock. Bring to the boil.

Cover and cook in a moderate oven, 325°F, Gas Mark 3 for 2½ hours. Stir in the tomatoes, olives and anchovy fillets. Cook for a further 30 minutes or until the meat is tender.

Taste and adjust the seasoning if necessary. Garnish with the chopped parsley before serving.

Serves 4-6

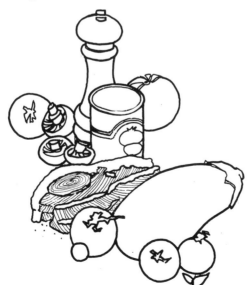

Pennywise Strogonoff

1 oz. (¼ cup) flour
salt
freshly ground black pepper
1 teaspoon dry mustard
1 lb. braising steak
2 oz. (¼ cup) margarine
2 onions, sliced
4 oz. (1 cup) mushrooms, sliced
½ pint (1¼ cups) beef stock
  (bouillon)

4 tablespoons (⅓ cup) tomato
  purée
5 fl. oz. (⅔ cup) natural
  (unflavored) yogurt
2-3 slices of bread, toasted and cut
  into triangles
sprig of fresh parsley to garnish

Combine the flour, salt, pepper and mustard. Cut the meat into thin strips about 1 inch × ½ inch. Toss in the seasoned flour to coat well. Heat the fat in a large frying pan over medium heat. Add the meat and fry quickly, stirring, until evenly browned. Lower the heat and add the onions and mushrooms. Cook for 3 minutes until the onions are soft, but not coloured.

Stir in the stock and tomato purée and bring to the boil, stirring constantly. Spoon the mixture into a shallow casserole dish. Cover and cook in a moderate oven, 350°F, Gas Mark 4 for 1½-1¾ hours.

Taste and adjust the seasoning, if necessary. Spoon the yogurt into the centre and arrange the toast triangles around the edge of the dish. Garnish with parsley and serve with boiled rice.
Serves 4

Country Casserole

2 oz. (¼ cup) beef dripping or lard
  (shortening)
1½ lb. stewing steak, cut into 1½
  inch cubes
4 onions, sliced
1 tablespoon flour
¾ pint (2 cups) beef stock
  (bouillon)
1 teaspoon dried mixed herbs

8 oz. carrots, peeled and sliced
1 lb. turnips, peeled and diced
freshly ground black pepper
1 teaspoon salt
1 teaspoon paprika
1 lb. potatoes, peeled and thinly
  sliced
1½ oz. (3T) butter

Heat the dripping or lard in a flameproof casserole over a high heat. Add the meat and onions and fry briskly until evenly and lightly browned. Lower the heat. Stir in the flour and cook for 2 minutes. Add the stock, herbs, carrots, turnips and seasonings. Bring to the boil, stirring.

Cover and cook in a moderate oven, 350°F, Gas Mark 4 for 2 hours. Remove the lid and arrange the sliced potatoes neatly over the surface. Dot with butter. Place on the top shelf of the oven and cook, uncovered, for a further 30 minutes or until browned.
Serves 4

PENNYWISE STROGONOFF *(Photograph: Chesswood Mushrooms)*

Mexican Pot Roast

2 tablespoons (3T) flour
1 teaspoon chilli powder
1 tablespoon paprika
salt
3 lb. rib of beef
4 tablespoons (⅓ cup) oil
2 onions, sliced
2 tablespoons (3T) tomato purée

¼ pint (⅔ cup) beef stock
  (bouillon)
6 cloves
1 tablespoon cornflour
  (cornstarch)
2 tablespoons (3T) water
2 × 15 oz. cans red kidney beans,
  drained

Combine the flour, chilli powder, paprika and salt. Coat the meat with the seasoned flour.

Heat the oil in a flameproof casserole over moderate heat. Add the meat and cook for 7 minutes, turning occasionally, until evenly browned. Remove. Add the onions to the casserole and fry for 3 minutes, stirring frequently, until just beginning to brown. Place the meat on top of the onions, add the tomato purée, stock and cloves. Bring to the boil.

Cover and cook in a moderate oven, 350°F, Gas Mark 4 for 2½ hours until the meat is tender. Transfer the meat to a serving dish and keep warm.

Blend the cornflour with the water. Stir into the cooking liquid and bring to the boil, stirring constantly. Add the beans and simmer for 3-4 minutes. Taste and adjust the seasoning. Pour over the meat before serving.
Serves 4-6

Goulash

4 tablespoons (⅓ cup) oil
2 lb. lean stewing steak, cut into 1
  inch cubes
2 onions, sliced
1 garlic clove, crushed
1 tablespoon flour
2 tablespoons (3T) paprika
1 teaspoon salt
½ teaspoon black pepper

1 teaspoon chopped fresh or ⅓
  teaspoon dried oregano
½ teaspoon caraway seeds,
  crushed
2 tablespoons (3T) tomato purée
1 pint (2½ cups) beef stock
  (bouillon)
1 lb. potatoes, peeled and sliced
¼ pint (⅔ cup) soured cream

Heat the oil in a flameproof casserole and add the meat. Fry, stirring frequently, until evenly browned. Remove the meat with a slotted spoon and add the onions and garlic to the casserole. Fry gently for 5 minutes until the onions are soft and transluscent.

Stir in the flour and paprika and cook, stirring, for 2 minutes. Add the salt, pepper, oregano, caraway seeds and tomato purée. Gradually stir in the stock and bring to the boil, stirring. Return the meat to the casserole, cover and cook in a moderate oven, 325°F, Gas Mark 3 for 1 hour.

Add the potato slices and cook for a further 1 hour. Stir in the soured cream and heat through, uncovered, for 5 minutes.
Serves 4-6

Paupiettes à l'Hongroise

3 oz. (⅓ cup) butter
4 onions, finely chopped
4 oz. (½ cup) lean veal, minced (ground)
2 tablespoons (3T) dry breadcrumbs
½ teaspoon celery salt
freshly ground black pepper
2½ teaspoons paprika
1½ teaspoons horseradish sauce
8 slices silverside (top round) of beef

8 slices streaky (fatty) bacon, derinded
⅓ pint (1 cup) red wine
2 tablespoons (3T) tomato purée
salt
4 oz. (1 cup) button mushrooms, sliced
¼ pint (⅔ cup) double (heavy) cream

Melt 1 oz. (2T) butter in a frying pan over moderate heat. Sauté 1 onion for 3-5 minutes until soft and translucent. Place in a bowl and add the veal, breadcrumbs, celery salt, pepper, ½ teaspoon paprika and the horseradish and beat well until thoroughly mixed.

Beat the slices of beef to flatten. Divide the filling evenly between them. Roll up the slices enclosing the filling. Wrap a slice of bacon around each one. Tie securely with string.

Melt the remaining butter in a flameproof casserole. Add the remaining onions and fry gently, stirring occasionally, for 5 minutes until soft and translucent, but do not allow to brown. Add the beef rolls and cook, turning occasionally until they are evenly browned.

Pour in the wine, then stir in the tomato purée, salt and remaining paprika. Bring the liquid to the boil. Cover the casserole and cook in a moderate oven, 350°F, Gas Mark 4 for 45 minutes.

Add the mushrooms and continue to cook for 15 minutes. Stir in the cream and cook for a further 5 minutes. Remove the string from the meat rolls. Taste and adjust the seasoning, if necessary. Serve with rice and a green vegetable.

Serves 4

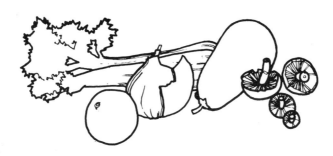

Beef Hot Pot

2 oz. (½ cup) flour
1 teaspoon salt
freshly ground black pepper
2 lb. braising steak, cut into 1 inch
 cubes
2 oz. (¼ cup) beef dripping
4 large onions, sliced
beef stock (bouillon)
1 turnip, peeled and diced

4 celery stalks, cut into 2 inch
 pieces
12 carrots, scraped and cut into
 quarters
1 green pepper, cored, seeded
 and sliced
12 small new potatoes, scrubbed
2 tablespoons (3T) chopped fresh
 parsley

Combine the flour, salt and pepper. Toss the meat cubes in the flour.

Melt the dripping in a large flameproof casserole over moderate heat. Add half the sliced onions and fry, stirring occasionally, for 10 minutes or until browned. Remove the onions with a slotted spoon. Increase the heat and fry the meat cubes quickly, a few at a time, until brown on all sides.

Return the meat and onions to the casserole. Pour in sufficient stock to cover. Add the remaining onions, turnip, celery and half the carrots. Cook covered, in a moderate oven, 325°F, Gas Mark 3 for 1½ hours.

Stir in the remaining carrots, green pepper and potatoes. Add ⅓ pint (1 cup) beef stock and the parsley. Continue cooking, covered, for 30 minutes. Taste and adjust the seasoning if necessary.
Serves 6

Oxtail Ragoût

1 oxtail, cut into joints
1½ oz. (⅓ cup) flour
salt
freshly ground black pepper
2 oz. (¼ cup) dripping or lard
 (shortening)
6 slices smoked streaky (fatty)
 bacon, derinded and chopped
2 onions, sliced

8 oz. (1½ cups) carrots, peeled
 and diced
4 sticks celery, diced
2 potatoes, peeled and diced
4 tomatoes, diced
2 tablespoons (3T) tomato purée
½ pint (1¼ cups) stock (bouillon)
bouquet garni
1 lemon, juice and grated rind

Coat the oxtail in the flour, seasoned with salt and pepper.

Melt the dripping or lard in a flameproof casserole over a low heat and sauté the bacon until the fat begins to run, but do not allow to brown. Remove the bacon with a slotted spoon. Add the onions, carrots and celery to the casserole and fry gently, stirring to prevent them sticking, until lightly browned. Take out the vegetables with a slotted spoon. Fry the oxtail in the remaining fat until well browned, stirring to prevent it sticking.

Stir in all other ingredients. Bring to the boil. Cover and cook in a cool oven, 300°F, Gas Mark 2 for 3 hours.

Remove the bouquet garni. Taste and adjust the seasoning, if necessary.
Serves 4-6

Braised Ox Tongue

1 small salted ox tongue
8 oz. (1 cup) smoked streaky (fatty) bacon, derinded and cut into ¼ inch pieces
2 tablespoons (3T) oil
1 large onion, diced
2 tablespoons (3T) flour
freshly ground black pepper
½ teaspoon fresh or pinch of dried basil
½ teaspoon fresh or pinch of dried thyme
½ teaspoon fresh or pinch of dried marjoram
3 tablespoons (¼ cup) tomato purée
¼ pint (⅔ cup) red wine
⅓ pint (1 cup) beef stock (bouillon)
6 oz. (1½ cups) button mushrooms, sliced
3 oz. (½ cup) black (ripe) olives, stoned

Soak the ox tongue for 12 hours in cold water, drain and place in a large pan. Cover with cold water, bring to the boil, then drain. Return the tongue to the pan and pour in sufficient fresh cold water to cover. Bring to the boil and simmer for 2½-3 hours or until tender.

Place the cooked tongue in a bowl of cold water, then peel off the skin. Remove bones and gristle. Cut the tongue into 1 inch slices and place in a casserole.

Fry the bacon in a saucepan over a very gentle heat until the fat begins to ooze. Remove the bacon with a slotted spoon and add the oil to the pan. Sauté the onion in the oil for 5 minutes until soft and transparent. Stir in the flour, seasoning, herbs and tomato purée. Replace the bacon in the pan. Gradually stir in the wine and stock. Bring to the boil, stirring all the time. Add the remaining ingredients, then pour the sauce over the tongue.

Cover and cook in a moderate oven, 350°F, Gas Mark 4 for 30 minutes. Remove the lid and continue to cook for a further 15 minutes.

Taste and adjust the seasoning, if necessary, before serving.

Serves 8-10

26

Tripe and Tomato Casserole

1 ½ lb. dressed tripe
2 tablespoons (3T) oil
2 tablespoons (3T) white vinegar
2 tablespoons (3T) lemon juice
2 oz. (¼ cup) butter
2 onions, sliced into rings
1 garlic clove, crushed
4 oz. (1 cup) button mushrooms,
  roughly chopped

4 oz. French beans
1 oz. (¼ cup) flour
14 oz. can tomatoes
1 tablespoon tomato purée
1 teaspoon dried basil
salt
freshly ground black pepper
3 oz. (¾ cup) fresh breadcrumbs

Cut the tripe into 2 inch pieces and place in a shallow dish. Mix the oil, vinegar and lemon juice together and pour over the tripe. Toss and leave to marinate for 1 hour.

In a small frying pan melt 1 oz. (2T) of the butter. Gently fry the onions and garlic, stirring continuously, for 3 minutes. Add the mushrooms and beans and continue cooking, stirring, for 3-4 minutes until the onions are soft, but not browned. With a slotted spoon, transfer the vegetables to a plate.

Sprinkle the flour into the pan juices and mix to a smooth paste. Drain the tomatoes and gradually add the tomato juice to the pan, stirring constantly. Bring to the boil, stirring. Stir in the tomatoes, tomato purée, basil and seasoning. Cook for 3 minutes.

Arrange half the onion, mushroom and bean mixture on the base of a greased, large shallow ovenproof dish. Sprinkle with half the breadcrumbs. With a slotted spoon, transfer the tripe to the dish, discarding the marinade. Pour over the tomato sauce. Arrange the remaining vegetables on top and sprinkle with the rest of the breadcrumbs. Dot with small pieces of butter.

Bake in a moderately hot oven, 375°F, Gas Mark 5 for 1 hour or until the tripe is tender. Taste and adjust the seasoning, if necessary. Serve immediately.

Serves 4

PORK CASSEROLES

Pork Fricassée

1½ lb. pork fillet (tenderloin) cut
  into 2 inch cubes
2 onions, chopped
¼ pint (⅔ cup) dry white wine
1 bay leaf
1 teaspoon dried thyme
salt

freshly ground black pepper
1 oz. (2T) butter
1 oz. (¼ cup) flour
¼ pint (⅔ cup) single (light) cream
4 oz. (1 cup) button mushrooms
sprig of fresh parsley to garnish

Place the pork, onions, wine, herbs and seasoning in a shallow casserole.
Cover and cook in a moderate oven, 325°F, Gas Mark 3 for 1¼ hours until
tender. Strain off the cooking liquor and reserve.

    Melt the butter in a saucepan over moderate heat and stir in the flour.
Stir in the cooking liquid and bring to the boil, stirring constantly. Simmer
for 2 minutes, stirring. Remove from the heat and add the cream and
mushrooms. Pour over the pork and return to the oven for 15 minutes.

    Taste and adjust the seasoning, if necessary. Garnish with parsley. Serve
the fricassée with saffron rice or plain boiled rice, if preferred.

Serves 4

Pork with Sage and Cream

1 oz. (¼ cup) flour
salt
freshly ground black pepper
½ teaspoon dry mustard
2 lb. pork, cut into 1 inch cubes
4 tablespoons (⅓ cup) oil
2 shallots, finely chopped
¾ pint (2 cups) chicken stock
  (bouillon)

1 tablespoon grated lemon rind
½ teaspoon dried savory
2 tablespoons (3T) chopped fresh
  or 2 teaspoons dried sage
4 oz. (1 cup) button mushrooms,
  sliced
¼ pint (⅔ cup) double (heavy)
  cream

Mix together the flour, salt, pepper and mustard. Toss the meat in the
seasoned flour.

    Heat the oil in a flameproof casserole and gently fry the shallots for 3-4
minutes until soft but not browned. Add the meat and cook, stirring, for 3-4
minutes. Stir in the stock and bring to the boil. Boil for 2 minutes then add
the lemon rind and herbs. Cover the casserole and place in a moderate
oven, 350°F, Gas Mark 4. Cook for 45 minutes.

    Stir in the mushrooms and cook for a further 15 minutes. Remove from
the oven and stir in the cream. Reheat but do not allow to boil. Taste and
adjust the seasoning, if necessary.

Serves 4-6

PORK FRICASSÉE *(Photograph: M.E.A.T.)*

Pork Valencia

5 lb. loin of pork, boned
1 large garlic clove, halved
1 teaspoon salt
freshly ground black pepper
½ teaspoon ground allspice
6 cloves
grated rind of 1 small orange
½ teaspoon dried coriander leaves
1 tablespoon finely chopped fresh
  or 1 teaspoon dried rosemary

1 oz. (2T) butter
½ pint (1¼ cups) sweet vermouth
4 large oranges, peeled and pith
  removed
1 tablespoon cornflour
  (cornstarch)
1 tablespoon water

Rub the pork with the garlic and discard the garlic clove. Unroll the pork so the inside is uppermost and sprinkle with the salt, black pepper, allspice, cloves, orange rind, coriander and rosemary. Reroll the meat and tie securely with string.

Melt the butter in a flameproof casserole over a medium heat and cook the pork for 10-12 minutes, turning frequently so that it becomes evenly browned. Pour the vermouth into the casserole and bring to the boil. With a sharp knife, cut the oranges into even slices. Add the orange slices to the casserole, cover and cook in a moderate oven, 350°F, Gas Mark 4 for 2½ hours or until the meat is tender.

Transfer the meat to a warmed serving dish and remove the string. With a slotted spoon, lift out the orange slices and arrange around the meat. Keep warm.

Skim off the excess fat from the cooking liquor and strain the liquid into a saucepan. Blend the cornflour with the water and stir into the sauce. Bring to the boil, stirring all the time. Cook, still stirring, for 3 minutes until the sauce is thickened and smooth. Taste and adjust the seasoning, if necessary. Pour enough sauce over the meat to coat it and serve the remainder in a warmed serving bowl.

Serves 8-10

Pork and Cabbage Braise

2 tablespoons (3T) oil
3 lb. shoulder of pork, boned and
  rolled
1 large onion, sliced
1 lb. firm white cabbage, finely
  sliced
2 oz. (⅓ cup) raisins

1 oz. (2T) brown sugar
½ teaspoon ground cloves
¼ pint (⅔ cup) dry (hard) cider
1 teaspoon celery salt
freshly ground black pepper
2 cooking apples, peeled, cored
  and sliced into rings

Heat the oil in a heavy frying pan and fry the meat for 5 minutes on all sides
until lightly and evenly browned. Remove.

Add the onion and cabbage to the pan and fry for 5 minutes, stirring
frequently, until lightly browned and softened. Add the raisins, sugar and
cloves and stir well.

Put the cabbage mixture into a large casserole, make a hollow in the
centre and put in the pork. Pour the cider over and sprinkle with the celery
salt and pepper. Cover and cook in a moderate oven, 325°F, Gas Mark 3
for 2 hours. Add the apple slices and cook, covered, for a further 30
minutes. Remove the meat, cut into slices and serve with the cabbage and
apple mixture.
Serves 4-6

Pork Piquant

4 tablespoons (⅓ cup) oil
4 slices bacon, derinded and
  chopped
2 onions, chopped
4 pork chops
2 oz. (½ cup) flour
salt
freshly ground black pepper
1 teaspoon paprika

1 pint (2½ cups) medium dry
  (hard) cider
1 tablespoon Worcestershire
  sauce
2 tomatoes, skinned and sliced
4 oz. (1 cup) button mushrooms,
  sliced
¼ pint (⅔ cup) soured cream

Heat the oil in a flameproof casserole and fry the bacon and onions for 3-4
minutes until the onions are soft but not brown. Remove with a slotted
spoon.

Trim the chops if necessary and coat liberally and evenly with flour.
Sprinkle salt, pepper and paprika over the meat. Fry for 4-5 minutes on
each side until lightly browned.

Return the onions and bacon to the casserole and pour in the cider and
Worcestershire sauce. Bring to the boil. Cover the casserole and cook in a
moderate oven, 325°F, Gas Mark 3 for 1 hour. Stir in the tomatoes and
mushrooms and continue to cook for 20 minutes.

Remove from the oven and stir in the soured cream and reheat but do
not allow to boil. Taste and adjust the seasoning if necessary.
Serves 4

Pork and Apple Casserole

3 tablespoons (¼ cup) flour
1 tablespoon dry mustard
salt
freshly ground black pepper
4 large or 8 small pork chops
2 oz. (¼ cup) butter
2 tablespoons (3T) oil

1 teaspoon dried sage
1 teaspoon dried thyme
1 bay leaf
1 onion, sliced
½ pint (1¼ cups) dry (hard) cider
1 cooking apple, cored and sliced
2 tomatoes, sliced

Combine flour, mustard, salt and pepper and coat the chops thoroughly with the seasoned flour.

Heat the butter and oil in a frying pan and gently fry the chops for 3 minutes on each side, until lightly browned. Transfer to a shallow casserole dish. Sprinkle with the herbs and arrange the sliced onion around the edge of the chops. Pour the cider over. Cover and cook in a moderate oven, 350°F, Gas Mark 4 for 1 hour.

Place the sliced apple and tomatoes on top of the onion and continue to cook for a further 15-20 minutes until the apple is tender. Remove the bay leaf before serving.
Serves 4

Pork Marseilles

1 lb. aubergines (eggplants)
salt
1½ lb. boned shoulder of pork, cut
  into 1 inch cubes
freshly ground black pepper
1 oz. (¼ cup) flour
5 tablespoons (6T) oil
1½ lb. tomatoes, peeled and
  quartered

1 large onion, chopped
1 clove garlic, crushed
1 teaspoon paprika
½ teaspoon dried oregano
1 red pepper, cored, seeded and
  sliced
1 green pepper, cored, seeded
  and sliced
2 oz. (⅓ cup) stuffed green olives

Slice the aubergines, place in a colander, sprinkle with salt and leave to drain for 30 minutes. Rinse and pat dry with kitchen paper.

Evenly coat the meat with seasoned flour, shaking off any excess. Heat the oil in a frying pan. When hot, add the meat and fry, stirring, for 4 minutes, until browned. Remove with a slotted spoon. Coat the aubergines in the remaining flour and fry for 3 minutes on each side. Remove. Add the tomatoes and onion to the pan and cook for 4 minutes. Stir in the garlic, paprika and oregano.

Arrange layers of pork, aubergines, tomato and onion mixture, sliced peppers and olives in a casserole. Cover and cook in a moderate oven, 325°F, Gas Mark 3 for 1¾-2 hours, until the meat is tender. Taste and adjust the seasoning, if necessary.
Serves 4

PORK AND APPLE CASSEROLE *(Photograph: M.E.A.T.)*

Porc à l'Indienne

Stuffing:

2 cooking apples, peeled, cored
  and sliced
2 tablespoons (3T) water
1 tablespoon castor (superfine)
  sugar
½ teaspoon dried sage
½ teaspoon dried thyme
salt
freshly ground black pepper
1 small onion, finely chopped
2 tablespoons (3T) fresh
  breadcrumbs

2 oz. (¼ cup) ham (cured), finely
  chopped
8 slices pork fillet (tenderloin)
2 tablespoons (3T) oil
½ teaspoon white pepper
¼ pint (⅔ cup) chicken stock
  (bouillon)
¼ pint (⅔ cup) white wine
2 tablespoons (3T) mild curry
  powder
½ oz. (1T) butter
½ oz. (2T) flour
¼ pint (⅔ cup) double (heavy)
  cream

Place the apples, water and sugar in a saucepan. Bring to the boil then simmer for 15 minutes or until soft. Beat in the herbs, ½ teaspoon salt, black pepper, onion, breadcrumbs and ham.

Spread the pork slices flat. Divide the stuffing evenly between the slices of meat. Roll up, enclosing the stuffing and secure with string.

Heat the oil gently in a flameproof casserole and fry the rolls for 6-8 minutes, turning frequently, until they are evenly browned. Stir in the white pepper, stock, wine and curry powder and heat until just boiling. Cover and cook in a moderate oven, 350°F, Gas Mark 4 for 45 minutes. Place the pork rolls on a warm serving dish and keep hot.

Place the casserole on top of the stove and bring the cooking liquor to the boil. Blend the butter and flour together to form a beurre manié and gradually stir into the cooking liquor. Continue to boil, stirring until the sauce thickens. Reduce the heat and stir in the cream. Do not reboil. Taste and adjust the seasoning, if necessary.

Pour the sauce over the meat and serve immediately.

Serves 4

New England Spare Rib Casserole

2 tablespoons (3T) golden
  (maple) syrup
¼ teaspoon cayenne pepper
salt
freshly ground black pepper

2 garlic cloves, crushed
2 tablespoons (3T) tomato purée
1 tablespoon French mustard
2 tablespoons (3T) lemon juice
4 spare rib pork chops

Combine the syrup, cayenne pepper, salt, pepper, garlic, tomato purée, mustard and lemon juice.

Put the spare ribs in an ovenproof dish and cook in a moderately hot oven, 400°F, Gas Mark 6 for 15 minutes. Pour off the excess fat and pour the syrup mixture over the meat.

Cover, reduce the oven temperature to moderate, 350°F, Gas Mark 4 and cook for 1 hour, basting occasionally. Remove the cover, baste again and increase the temperature to 400°F, Gas Mark 6. Cook for 15 minutes until the ribs are glazed and brown.

Transfer the ribs to a warmed serving dish and pour the sauce over.
Serves 4

Pork Almendrado

4 pork chops
4 oz. (1 cup) blanched almonds,
  toasted and chopped
1 oz. (¼ cup) flour
salt
freshly ground black pepper
4 tablespoons (⅓ cup) oil

2 oz. (½ cup) onions, chopped
2 oz. (½ cup) button mushrooms,
  sliced
½ pint (1¼ cups) chicken stock
  (bouillon)
¼ pint (⅔ cup) dry sherry
¼ pint (⅔ cup) single (light) cream

With the point of a sharp knife, make a slit lengthwise through each chop. Fill with almonds. Mix together the flour, salt and pepper. Coat the chops in the seasoned flour.

Heat the oil in a heavy frying pan and gently fry the chops for 4-5 minutes on each side until lightly browned. Transfer to a casserole dish. Add the onions to the fat remaining in the pan and gently fry for 3 minutes, stirring all the time. Add the mushrooms and cook for a further 2 minutes, turning occasionally to prevent the vegetables browning.

Pour in the stock and bring to the boil. Remove from the heat and stir in the sherry. Pour over the meat. Cover the casserole and cook in a moderate oven, 350°F, Gas Mark 4 for 1 hour.

Pour in the cream and heat through. Taste and adjust the seasoning, if necessary.
Serves 4

Pork Chops in Tomato and Onion Sauce

1 oz. (2T) dripping
4-6 loin or spare rib chops
2 onions, sliced
1 lb. tomatoes, roughly chopped
¼ pint (⅔ cup) chicken stock
  (bouillon)

1 bay leaf
bouquet garni
salt
freshly ground black pepper
sprigs of fresh parsley to garnish

Heat the dripping in a large frying pan and fry the chops for 5 minutes on each side or until evenly browned. Remove from the pan.

Add the onions to the fat remaining in the pan and sauté over low heat until soft and translucent. Stir in the tomatoes, stock, herbs and seasoning to taste. Bring to the boil and simmer for 5 minutes.

Spoon the tomato and onion mixture into a shallow casserole and lay the pork chops on top. Cover and cook in a moderate oven, 350°F, Gas Mark 4 for 1-1¼ hours, basting occasionally.

Remove the bay leaf and bouquet garni before serving. Garnish the chops with sprigs of parsley.

Serves 4-6

Pork and Bean Casserole

1 oz. (¼ cup) flour
1 teaspoon salt
freshly ground black pepper
1 teaspoon dry mustard
2 lb. pork, cut into 2 inch cubes
2 tablespoons (3T) oil
2 onions, sliced
1 lb. (3 cups) carrots, peeled and
  sliced

2 green peppers, cored, seeded
  and sliced
¾ pint (2 cups) chicken stock
  (bouillon)
1½ teaspoons chopped fresh sage
½ teaspoon chopped fresh thyme
1 tablespoon grated lemon rind
8 oz. cooked haricot (navy) beans
  or red kidney beans

Combine flour, salt, pepper and mustard. Toss meat in the seasoned flour to coat thoroughly.

Heat the oil in a large frying pan over a moderate heat and fry the meat, turning occasionally, for 5 minutes, until lightly and evenly browned. Add the vegetables and fry for a further 3-4 minutes, turning occasionally until softened but not browned.

Add the stock, herbs and lemon rind. Bring to the boil. Transfer to a deep casserole. Cover and cook in a moderate oven, 325°F, Gas Mark 3 for 1½ hours.

Stir in the beans and cook for a further 30 minutes. Taste and adjust the seasoning, if necessary.

Serves 6

Meat Ball and Onion Casserole

1 egg, beaten
3 tablespoons (¼ cup) milk
2 oz. (1 cup) fresh white
  breadcrumbs
2 lb. lean pork, minced (ground)
1 tablespoon finely chopped fresh
  or 1 teaspoon dried dill
1 tablespoon flour
¼ teaspoon celery salt
½ teaspoon salt
½ teaspoon white pepper

2 oz. (¼ cup) butter or margarine
2 large onions, thinly sliced into
  rings
1 tablespoon cornflour
  (cornstarch)
½ pint (1¼ cups) chicken stock
  (bouillon)
2 tablespoons (3T) lemon juice
2 tablespoons (3T) Madeira
  (optional)

In a large mixing bowl, beat the egg with the milk. Add the breadcrumbs, pork, dill, flour and seasonings. Mix and knead until evenly blended. With lightly floured hands, shape into approximately 20 balls, about 1½ inches in diameter.

In a flameproof casserole, melt 1 oz. (2T) of the butter or margarine, add the onions and cook, stirring occasionally, for 5-7 minutes until soft but not brown. Remove, using a slotted spoon.

Add the remaining fat to the casserole. Put in the meat balls, a few at a time and fry, turning so they cook evenly, for 6-8 minutes. Take out the meat balls and set aside.

Blend the cornflour with a little of the stock then stir into the casserole juices together with the remaining stock, lemon juice and Madiera, if used. Bring to the boil, stirring constantly. Take off the heat. Add the onions and meat balls and place the casserole in a moderately hot oven, 375°F, Gas Mark 5. Cook for 45 minutes.

Transfer the meat balls to a warmed serving dish. Taste the sauce and adjust the seasoning, if necessary. Pour over the meat balls. Serve with rice.

Serves 4-6

Pork Muscadet

2 lb. seedless green (white) grapes
4 lb. shoulder of pork, boned and
  rolled
salt
freshly ground black pepper
1 teaspoon ground coriander
12 juniper berries, crushed
1 clove garlic, crushed
2 small onions, finely chopped
1 tablespoon Worcestershire
  sauce

2 oz. (¼ cup) butter
3 tablespoons (¼ cup) gin
1 tablespoon cornflour
  (cornstarch)
¼ pint (⅔ cup) dry white wine
Garnish:
1½ oz. (3T) butter
1½ lb. seedless green (white)
  grapes

Purée the grapes and sieve to extract the juice. Cut the meat into slices. Rub the pork with salt and pepper and place in a large dish. Pour the grape juice over the meat and add the coriander, juniper berries, garlic, 1 onion and the Worcestershire sauce. Leave to marinate at room temperature for 8 hours or overnight.

Remove the pork from the marinade and drain thoroughly. Reserve the marinade. Heat the butter in a large flameproof casserole over moderate heat and fry the remaining onion for 3-4 minutes until soft and translucent but not browned. Add the pork slices and cook for 3-4 minutes on each side to brown.

In a separate saucepan, boil the reserved marinade until it has reduced by half. Pour over the pork. Cover the casserole and place in a moderate oven, 350°F, Gas Mark 4. Cook for 1 hour until the meat is tender.

Meanwhile, prepare the garnish. Melt the butter in a pan, add the grapes and cook, turning frequently, for 6-8 minutes until lightly browned.

Warm the gin over a low heat for 2 minutes. Pour over the pork and ignite. When the flames die down, transfer the meat to a warmed serving dish. Keep warm.

Blend the cornflour with 1 tablespoon of the wine. Skim the excess fat from the casserole. Stir in the dissolved cornflour and remaining wine. Bring to the boil, stirring constantly. Simmer for 3 minutes until the sauce is thick and smooth. Taste and adjust the seasoning, if necessary.

Pour the sauce over the pork and arrange the garnish around the meat. Serve with rice or potatoes and a fresh green vegetable such as broccoli or Brussels sprouts.
Serves 6-8

LAMB CASSEROLES

Lamb Provençal

1½ lb. boned leg of lamb, cut into
  1 inch cubes
salt
freshly ground black pepper
2 oz. (¼ cup) butter
2 tablespoons (3T) oil
2 onions, chopped
1 teaspoon paprika
1 garlic clove, crushed
12 oz. tomatoes or 14 oz. can
  tomatoes, drained

1 tablespoon tomato purée
1 teaspoon dried mixed herbs
1 bay leaf
½ pint (1¼ cups) dry white wine
4 oz. (1 cup) button mushrooms,
  sliced
1 green pepper, cored, seeded
  and sliced

Trim any excess fat and skin from the meat. Rub with salt and pepper. Heat the butter and oil in a flameproof casserole over moderate heat and fry the lamb cubes, stirring to prevent sticking, until evenly browned. Remove the meat with a slotted spoon.

Add the onions to the casserole and fry gently for 4 minutes until soft but not browned. Stir in the paprika and garlic and cook for 2 minutes.

Peel and chop the tomatoes, if using fresh ones. Stir the tomatoes, purée, herbs and wine into the casserole. Bring to the boil. Add the lamb, cover and cook in a moderate oven, 350°F, Gas Mark 4 for 45 minutes.

Add the mushrooms and green pepper and continue to cook for 20 minutes. Remove the lid, stir well and cook for a further 5-10 minutes. Check the seasoning and remove the bay leaf before serving.
Serves 4

Lemon Braised Lamb

4 tablespoons (⅓ cup) oil
salt and black pepper
2 teaspoons grated lemon rind
2½ oz. (⅔ cup) flour
2 lb. boned shoulder of lamb, cut
  into 1½ inch cubes
1 garlic clove, crushed
¼ pint (⅔ cup) dry white wine

1 pint (2½ cups) stock (bouillon)
1 bay leaf
1 teaspoon fresh or ⅓ teaspoon
  dried thyme
2 egg yolks
2½ teaspoons lemon juice
2 tablespoons (3T) chopped fresh
  parsley

Heat the oil in a flameproof casserole. Combine the salt, pepper, lemon rind and flour and coat the lamb well. Add the meat to the oil and fry, stirring frequently, until golden brown all over; about 8 minutes. Add the garlic and cook for 2 minutes. Gradually pour in the wine and stock, stirring constantly. Bring to the boil, stirring. Simmer for 2 minutes.

Add the bay leaf and thyme, cover and place in a moderate oven, 350°F, Gas Mark 4. Cook for 1 hour or until the meat is tender. Transfer the lamb to a serving dish and strain the liquor into a saucepan. Skim off any excess fat.

Blend the egg yolks with the lemon juice, then stir in 2 tablespoons (3T) of the hot sauce. Gradually add a little more and blend well to give a smooth texture. Stir this into the saucepan and bring to the boil, stirring constantly. Cook gently, stirring, until the sauce has thickened.

Taste and adjust the seasoning, if necessary. Pour over the lamb and sprinkle with the parsley to garnish. Serve with new potatoes.
Serves 4-6

Surprise Casserole

1 lb. boned shoulder of lamb, cut
  into 1 inch cubes
salt
freshly ground black pepper
4 tablespoons (⅓ cup) oil
3 onions, sliced
2 teaspoons clear honey

½ teaspoon ground cinnamon
½ teaspoon dried mixed herbs
½ teaspoon grated nutmeg
8 oz. can tomatoes
2 oz. (½ cup) mushrooms, sliced
4 slices brown bread, buttered and
  quartered

Trim the lamb and rub with salt and pepper. Heat the oil in a large frying pan over a moderate heat and fry the lamb, stirring, until browned. Transfer the meat to an ovenproof dish.

Fry the onions in the oil remaining in the pan for 5 minutes until soft but not browned. Stir in the remaining ingredients, except the bread, and bring to the boil. Pour over the meat, cover and cook in a moderate oven, 350°F, Gas Mark 4 for 1 hour. Taste and adjust seasoning, if necessary.

Arrange the bread slices neatly on top and return to the oven for 30 minutes until the bread is crisp.
Serves 4

Liver Casserole

1½ lb. lambs' liver, sliced
3 tablespoons (¼ cup) lemon juice
salt and pepper
1 oz. (¼ cup) flour
4 tablespoons (⅓ cup) oil
2 onions, sliced
4 oz. (1 cup) button mushrooms, sliced
14 oz. can tomatoes, drained
1 teaspoon paprika
1 teaspoon dried sage
1 teaspoon dried basil
2 tablespoons (3T) Worcestershire sauce
1 green pepper, cored, seeded and sliced
1 tablespoon chopped fresh parsley

Sprinkle the liver with lemon juice and leave for 30 minutes, turning occasionally. Dry well and coat with the seasoned flour.

Heat the oil in a frying pan and fry the liver for 2 minutes on each side. Transfer to a casserole. Fry the onions in the oil remaining in the pan for 5 minutes until soft but not browned. Add the mushrooms and cook for a further 2 minutes. Add the remaining ingredients and bring to the boil. Pour over the liver. Cover the casserole and cook in a moderate oven, 350°F, Gas Mark 4 for 30 minutes, or until the liver is tender.

Taste and adjust the seasoning, if necessary.

Serves 4

Grecian Lamb

2 aubergines (eggplants), sliced
salt
5 tablespoons (6T) oil
2 lb. boned leg of lamb, cut into 1 inch cubes
2 teaspoons coriander seeds, coarsely crushed
1 large onion, sliced
1 garlic clove, crushed
2 tablespoons (3T) fresh mint, chopped
1 lb. tomatoes, peeled and chopped
freshly ground black pepper
5 fl. oz. (⅔ cup) natural (unflavored) yogurt

Place the aubergines in a colander and sprinkle with 2 teaspoons salt. Leave to drain for 30 minutes, then dry on kitchen paper.

Heat the oil in a large frying pan. Add half the lamb cubes and fry gently until evenly browned. Remove with a slotted spoon and place in a casserole. Repeat with the rest of the lamb, adding the coriander seeds before frying.

Add the onion to the fat remaining in the pan and sauté until golden. Add the garlic and mint and cook for 1 minute. Add the aubergines and fry, stirring frequently, for 10 minutes. Stir in the tomatoes and seasoning to taste. Pour over the meat and cook in a moderate oven, 350°F, Gas Mark 4 for 1 hour.

Stir in the yogurt and continue to cook for 5-10 minutes. Taste and adjust the seasoning, if necessary.

Serves 6

Country Style Lamb Casserole

2 tablespoons (3T) flour
salt
freshly ground black pepper
1 teaspoon dry mustard
1½ lb. best end of neck lamb
  cutlets (rib chops)
2 tablespoons (3T) oil
3 onions, sliced

3 carrots, sliced
2 sticks celery, chopped
4 oz. (1 cup) swede, chopped
2 parsnips, chopped
½ teaspoon dried thyme
¾ pint (2 cups) stock (bouillon)
4-6 button onions
1 tablespoon clear honey

Combine the flour, salt, pepper and mustard. Coat the chops with the seasoned flour and shake off any excess. Reserve this flour.

Heat the oil in a flameproof casserole over moderate heat. Add the chops and fry for 5 minutes on each side until golden brown. Take the chops out of the casserole, add the onions, carrots and celery and fry, stirring occasionally, for 3 minutes. Add the swede and parsnips and fry for a further 2 minutes.

Return the chops to the casserole and sprinkle with the thyme and seasoned flour. Add the stock, button onions and honey. Bring to the boil, stirring. Cover and cook in a moderate oven, 350°F, Gas Mark 4 for 1½ hours or until the meat is tender.

Taste and adjust the seasoning, if necessary, before serving.
Serves 4

Spring Lamb

2 lb. boned shoulder of lamb, cut
  into 2 inch cubes
1 oz. (2T) butter
6 spring onions (scallions), sliced
1 garlic clove, crushed
¼ pint (⅔ cup) dry white wine
¾ pint (2 cups) chicken stock
  (bouillon)

1½ lb. new potatoes
salt
freshly ground black pepper
1 teaspoon grated lemon rind
2 tablespoons (3T) chopped fresh
  parsley
4 tablespoons (⅓ cup) chopped
  fresh mint

Trim the meat and remove any excess fat and skin. Melt the butter in a large frying pan over low heat. Add the meat cubes and fry for 5 minutes, stirring frequently, until lightly browned all over. Remove with a slotted spoon and transfer to a casserole.

Add the onions and garlic to the pan and fry, stirring, until transparent and soft. Pour in the wine and stock, stirring to dislodge any sediment. Add the potatoes and bring to the boil. Sprinkle in the salt, pepper, lemon rind and herbs.

Pour over the lamb, cover and place the casserole in a moderate oven, 350°F, Gas Mark 4. Cook for 1 hour or until the meat is tender. Taste and adjust the seasoning, if necessary. Serve immediately with fresh peas.
Serves 6

Lamb and Sweetcorn Supper

4 loin or chump lamb chops
salt
freshly ground black pepper
4 tablespoons (⅓ cup) oil
4 tablespoons (⅓ cup) chopped
  pimento
2 tablespoons (3T) tomato purée

10 oz. can sweetcorn kernels,
  drained
¼ teaspoon cayenne pepper
1 tablespoon chopped fresh
  chives
½ pint (1¼ cups) tomato juice

Rub the chops with salt and pepper. Heat the oil in a flameproof casserole over a moderate heat. Fry the chops for 3-4 minutes on each side. Add the remaining ingredients and bring to the boil. Cover the casserole and cook in a moderate oven, 350°F, Gas Mark 4 for 45 minutes.

Taste and adjust the seasoning if necessary before serving.
Serves 4

Lamb with Rosemary

2 lb. shoulder of lamb, cut into 1
  inch cubes
2 lemons, juice and grated rind
1 tablespoon white wine vinegar
2 tablespoons (3T) chopped fresh
  rosemary
4 sprigs of fresh parsley
4 tablespoons (⅓ cup) oil
2 oz. (½ cup) flour

¾ pint (2 cups) milk
bouquet garni
6 peppercorns, crushed
6 coriander seeds, crushed
1 tablespoon grated orange rind
1 oz. (2T) butter
2 teaspoons soft brown (light)
  sugar

Place the meat cubes, lemon juice, rind, vinegar, 1 tablespoon rosemary and the parsley sprigs in a bowl. Toss the mixture and leave to marinate for 2 hours, basting frequently.

With a slotted spoon remove the meat. Strain the marinade, reserving the liquid but discard the flavourings. Dry the meat.

Heat the oil in a flameproof casserole over moderate heat and fry the meat, turning frequently, for 6-8 minutes until lightly and evenly browned. Stir in the flour then gradually add the milk, stirring and bring to the boil. Simmer for 2 minutes.

Add the bouquet garni, peppercorns, coriander seeds and remaining rosemary. Stir well then add the orange rind. Place in a moderate oven, 350°F, Gas Mark 4. Cook for 45 minutes.

Melt the butter in a small frying pan over moderate heat and add the sugar. Bring to the boil then cook, stirring constantly, until caramelized. Add to the casserole with the marinade and cook for a further 30 minutes.

Transfer the meat to a serving dish. Strain the sauce into a saucepan and boil to reduce and thicken slightly. Taste and adjust the seasoning if necessary. Pour over the meat before serving.
Serves 4-6

Sweet Pepper Casserole

salt
freshly ground black pepper
1 teaspoon dry mustard
1 lb. boned shoulder of lamb, cut
  into 1 inch cubes
4 tablespoons (⅓ cup) oil
1 lb. (4 cups) onions, chopped
1 green pepper, cored, seeded
  and cut into strips
½ red pepper, cored, seeded and
  cut into strips

8 oz. can tomatoes
dash of Tabasco sauce
1 tablespoon Worcestershire
  sauce
1 teaspoon brown sugar
1 teaspoon fresh or ⅓ teaspoon
  dried thyme
¼ pint (⅔ cup) stock (bouillon)
4 new potatoes, peeled and sliced
  into rounds

Mix together salt, pepper and mustard. Trim the meat then rub with the seasonings.

Heat the oil over a moderate heat and fry the meat and onions, stirring, until evenly browned. Add the peppers, tomatoes, sauces, sugar, thyme and stock and bring to the boil. Simmer for 2 minutes. Pour into a casserole and top with the potatoes. Cover and cook in a moderate oven, 350°F, Gas Mark 4 for 1 hour or until the meat is tender. Taste and adjust the seasoning, if necessary.

Serves 4

Spiced Lamb

2 lb. leg of lamb, cut into 2 inch
  cubes
salt
freshly ground black pepper
4 tablespoons (⅓ cup) oil
1 garlic clove, crushed
3 large onions, thinly sliced
1 bay leaf
¼ teaspoon ground cloves

¼ teaspoon ground ginger
¾ pint (2 cups) white stock
  (bouillon)
3 tablespoons (¼ cup)
  breadcrumbs, made from
  pumpernickel or black bread
1 tablespoon capers
2 tablespoons (3T) lemon juice
grated rind of 1 lemon

Rub the lamb with salt and pepper. Heat the oil in a frying pan and fry the meat for about 5 minutes until evenly browned. Transfer to a casserole.

Add the garlic and onions to the frying pan and sauté gently for 5-7 minutes until the onions are soft and translucent but not brown. Add the bay leaf, cloves and ginger and mix well. Stir in the stock and bring to the boil.

Pour over the lamb and cover the casserole. Cook in a moderate oven, 350°F, Gas Mark 4 for 30 minutes. Stir in the breadcrumbs, capers, lemon juice and rind and cook for a further 45 minutes. Remove the lid and cook for 15 minutes until the meat is tender.

Taste and adjust the seasoning, if necessary.

Serves 6

Lancashire Hot Pot

2 lb. middle neck of lamb cutlets
  (rib chops)
3 tablespoons (¼ cup) flour
salt and pepper
4 onions, sliced
2 lamb's kidneys, cored and sliced
8 oz. (1½ cups) carrots, diced

1½ lb. potatoes, sliced
¾ pint (2 cups) light stock
  (bouillon)
1 bay leaf
½ teaspoon dried marjoram
½ teaspoon dried thyme

Trim off any excess fat from the lamb and coat with the flour, seasoned with salt and pepper.

Place layers of meat, onions, kidneys, carrots and potatoes in a large casserole, seasoning each layer lightly with salt and pepper. Finish with a layer of potatoes. Heat the stock and sprinkle in the herbs. Pour into the casserole and cook, covered, in a moderate oven, 350°F, Gas Mark 4 for 2 hours. Remove the lid and cook for a further 30 minutes to brown the potatoes.

Serves 4

Lambs' Tongues in Sweet and Sour Sauce

4 lambs' tongues
salt and pepper
2 tablespoons (3T) cornflour
  (cornstarch)
½ pint (1¼ cups) dry (hard) cider
4 tablespoons (⅓ cup) brown
  sugar

2 tablespoons (3T) cranberry
  sauce
2 tablespoons (3T) soy sauce
4 tablespoons (⅓ cup) vinegar

Soak the tongues for 1-2 hours in lightly salted water. Drain and place in a large saucepan. Add seasoning and enough water to cover, bring to the boil and simmer for 2 hours or until tender. Drain thoroughly. Cut the tongues in half lengthwise and place in a casserole.

Blend the cornflour with a little of the cider in a saucepan, then pour in the remaining cider, sugar, cranberry sauce and soy sauce.

Bring to the boil, stirring constantly, and simmer for 2 minutes. Stir in the vinegar. Pour the sauce over the tongues. Cover and cook in a moderate oven, 350°F, Gas Mark 4 for 35 minutes. Remove the lid and cook for a further 5 minutes.

Taste and adjust the seasoning, if necessary. Serve with buttered noodles.

Serves 4

LANCASHIRE HOT POT *(Photograph: New Zealand Lamb Information Bureau)*

VEAL CASSEROLES

Savoury Escalopes

Sauce:
4 tablespoons (⅓ cup) oil
2 onions, thinly sliced
1 garlic clove, crushed
2 teaspoons finely chopped fresh
  parsley
1 teaspoon chopped fresh or ⅓
  teaspoon dried basil
16 oz. can tomatoes
salt
freshly ground black pepper
3 oz. (¾ cup) Cheddar cheese,
  finely grated

Stuffing:
4 oz. (½ cup) butter
1 small onion, finely chopped
2 oz. (½ cup) button mushrooms,
  finely chopped
2 oz. (¼ cup) ham (cured), finely
  chopped
¼ teaspoon dried oregano
2 tablespoons (3T) dry
  breadcrumbs
1 teaspoon grated lemon rind
2 tablespoons (3T) lemon juice
4 veal escalopes, pounded thin
2 oz. (½ cup) Emmenthal cheese,
  grated

Heat the oil for the sauce in a large saucepan over a moderate heat. Fry the onions and garlic, stirring occasionally, for 5 minutes until soft but not browned. Add the parsley, basil, tomatoes with their juice, salt and pepper. Mix well and bring to the boil. Simmer gently for 30 minutes, stirring occasionally, until the sauce has reduced slightly and thickened. Remove from the heat and stir in the cheese.

Meanwhile prepare the stuffing. Melt 1 oz. (2T) butter in a pan over low heat. Gently sauté the onion, mushrooms, ham and oregano for 3 minutes. Stir in the breadcrumbs, lemon rind, juice and seasoning.

Lay the escalopes on a working surface and evenly divide the stuffing mixture between them. Roll each one up, enclosing the stuffing and tie with string to make parcels. Melt the remaining butter and fry the veal for 8-10 minutes, turning occasionally, until evenly browned. Place in a casserole.

Pour the sauce over the veal. Cover and place in a moderate oven, 350°F, Gas Mark 4. Cook for 1 hour or until the meat is tender. Taste and adjust the seasoning, if necessary.

Discard the string. Sprinkle the Emmenthal over the casserole and place under a hot grill until golden brown.
Serves 4

Blanquette of Veal

2 lb. breast of veal, cut into 2 inch
  cubes
2 carrots, peeled and diced
1 onion, sliced
1 stick celery, sliced
1 teaspoon chopped fresh or ⅓
  teaspoon dried thyme
1 bay leaf
3 sprigs fresh parsley, chopped
grated rind of 1 lemon
salt

freshly ground black pepper
2 oz. (¼ cup) butter
2 onions, finely diced
8 oz. (2 cups) mushrooms,
  quartered
1½ oz. (⅓ cup) flour
2 egg yolks
¼ pint (⅔ cup) single (light) cream
1 teaspoon lemon juice
few lemon slices to garnish

Place the veal in a flameproof casserole. Add the carrots, onion, celery, herbs, lemon rind and seasoning. Pour in sufficient water to just cover the veal. Bring to the boil and skim.

Transfer the casserole to the oven and cook at 325°F, Gas Mark 3 for 1 hour or until the meat is tender. Remove the meat and keep warm. Strain the liquor, discarding the vegetables. Boil the liquor until reduced to approximately 1 pint (2½ cups). Reserve.

Melt 1 oz. (2T) of the butter in a saucepan and add the onions and mushrooms. Sauté gently until the onions are soft and translucent but not brown. Remove the vegetables with a slotted spoon and reserve.

Melt the remaining butter in the pan. Sprinkle in the flour and cook for 1 minute; do not allow the roux to brown. Gradually add the reserved stock and bring to the boil, stirring. Continue to cook, stirring, until the sauce has thickened.

Beat the egg yolks with the cream. Blend 2 tablespoons (3T) of the hot sauce into this mixture, then gradually add the remaining sauce. Return to the pan and heat through, stirring, but do not allow to boil.

Add the veal, mushrooms, onions and lemon juice. Taste and adjust the seasoning, if necessary, and remove the bay leaf. Garnish with lemon slices before serving.

Serves 6

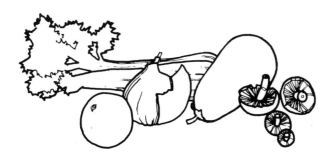

Veal Olives

½ × 4 oz. packet parsley and
  thyme stuffing mix
4 slices bacon, derinded and
  chopped
1 lemon, grated rind and juice
2 onions, finely chopped
4 large veal escalopes, pounded
  thin

1 oz. (2T) butter
2 tomatoes, peeled and chopped
¼ pint (⅔ cup) chicken stock
  (bouillon)
salt
freshly ground black pepper

Combine the stuffing mix with ¼ pint (⅔ cup) water and leave to stand for 10 minutes. Add the bacon, lemon rind and 1 chopped onion and mix well. Sprinkle the lemon juice over the escalopes and spread evenly with stuffing. Roll up the escalopes, enclosing filling and tie securely with string.

Melt the butter in a frying pan over a gentle heat and fry the remaining onion for 3 minutes until translucent and just softened. Add the veal olives and brown evenly on all sides. Place the veal and onion in a casserole, add the tomatoes, stock and seasoning. Cover and cook in a moderate oven, 350°F, Gas Mark 4 for 50 minutes or until the meat is tender. Taste and adjust the seasoning. Serve with creamed potatoes and Brussels sprouts.
Serves 4

Veal with Tomatoes and Garlic

1½ lb. shin (shank) of veal
8 oz. tomatoes, skinned and
  chopped
salt
freshly ground black pepper
1 tablespoon brown sugar
½ teaspoon dried basil
½ teaspoon dried marjoram
1 teaspoon grated orange rind

1 teaspoon oil
¼ pint (⅔ cup) veal or chicken
  stock (bouillon)
3 tablespoons (¼ cup)
  breadcrumbs
1 garlic clove, finely chopped
2 teaspoons grated lemon rind
1 tablespoon chopped fresh
  parsley

Ask your butcher to cut the veal into 3 inch pieces.

Put the tomatoes, salt, pepper, sugar, basil, marjoram and orange rind into a saucepan. Bring to the boil, lower the heat slightly and cook until reduced to a pulp.

Heat oil in a flameproof casserole, add meat and cook for 4-5 minutes, stirring occasionally, until browned. Pour in the tomato mixture and stock and simmer, uncovered, for 15 minutes. Cover and cook in a moderate oven, 325°F, Gas Mark 3 for 1 hour.

Mix the breadcrumbs with the garlic, lemon rind and parsley and sprinkle over the top of the casserole. Continue to cook for another 15 minutes, uncovered. Taste and adjust the seasoning, if necessary, before serving.
Serves 4

VEAL OLIVES *(Photograph: M.E.A.T.)*

POULTRY CASSEROLES

Chicken with Asparagus and Prawns (Shrimp)

2 oz. (¼ cup) butter
5 lb. oven ready chicken, cut into 8
  serving pieces
2 onions, finely chopped
3 tablespoons (¼ cup) flour
¾ pint (2 cups) chicken stock
  (bouillon)
½ teaspoon paprika
salt
freshly ground black pepper

½ teaspoon dry mustard
2 tablespoons (3T) Madeira
1 bay leaf
1 lb. can asparagus, drained
8 oz. (1¼ cups) peeled prawns
  (shrimp)
¼ pint (⅔ cup) double (heavy)
  cream
few sprigs of fresh parsley to
  garnish

Melt the butter in a large flameproof casserole over a moderate heat. Fry 2
or 3 of the chicken portions at a time, for 4-5 minutes on each side until
golden brown. Remove from the casserole and cook the remaining joints.
Remove and set aside.

Add the onions to the casserole and sauté over low heat until soft and
transparent. Stir in the flour, then gradually add the stock, stirring. Sprinkle
in the paprika, salt, pepper and mustard. Bring to the boil, stirring. Take off
the heat and pour in the Madeira, then add the chicken and bay leaf.
Cover and cook in a moderate oven, 350°F, Gas Mark 4 for 30 minutes.

Stir in the asparagus and prawns and cook for a further 30 minutes. Stir
in the cream and heat through but do not allow to boil. Remove the bay
leaf, taste and correct the seasoning. Serve garnished with the parsley
sprigs.
Serves 8

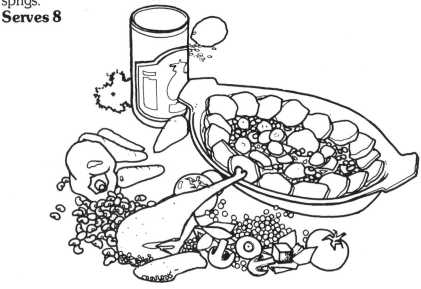

Country Chicken Casserole

4 chicken joints
salt
freshly ground black pepper
1 oz. (¼ cup) flour
3 tablespoons (¼ cup) oil
4 slices smoked streaky (fatty)
  bacon, derinded and diced
8 oz. (1½ cups) carrots, peeled
  and sliced into rounds

1 onion, sliced
4 tomatoes, peeled and sliced
2 oz. (5T) long grain rice
½ pint (1¼ cups) chicken stock
  (bouillon)
8 oz. (1½ cups) frozen peas

Rub the chicken joints with salt and pepper. Coat with the flour. Heat the oil in a large frying pan over moderate heat and fry the joints, two at a time, for 5-7 minutes until evenly browned. Transfer to a large casserole.

Add the bacon, carrots, onion, tomatoes, rice and seasoning to the pan juices and mix well. Add this mixture to the casserole. Pour over the stock. Cover and cook in a moderately hot oven, 375°F, Gas Mark 5 for 45 minutes. Stir in the peas then return to the oven for a further 15 minutes or until the chicken is tender and the vegetables are cooked. Taste and adjust the seasoning, if necessary, before serving.
Serves 4

Mediterranean Chicken

2 oz. (¼ cup) butter
4 chicken joints
1 onion, sliced
8 oz. (2 cups) button mushrooms,
  sliced
½ oz. (2T) flour
½ pint (1¼ cups) chicken stock
  (bouillon)
salt

freshly ground black pepper
1 teaspoon dried oregano
1 teaspoon dried marjoram
1 green pepper, cored, seeded
  and sliced
4 large ripe tomatoes, peeled and
  quartered
2 oz. (⅓ cup) stuffed olives

Melt the butter in a flameproof casserole over a low heat. Add the chicken joints and fry for 5 minutes on each side until lightly browned. Remove the chicken.

Add the onion to the casserole and cook gently for 5 minutes, stirring occasionally, until softened but not browned. Add the mushrooms and cook for a further 1 minute. Blend in the flour and cook for 1 minute, then stir in the stock. Bring to the boil, stirring constantly and simmer for 2 minutes. Stir in the salt, pepper, herbs and green pepper and return the chicken joints to the casserole.

Cover and cook in a moderate oven, 350°F, Gas Mark 4 for 1 hour. Add the tomatoes and stuffed olives and cook for a further 10 minutes. Taste and adjust the seasoning, if necessary.
Serves 4

Normandy Chicken

4 chicken portions
salt
freshly ground black pepper
4 tablespoons (⅓ cup) oil
2 onions, sliced
1 stick celery, chopped
3 slices bacon, diced
1 oz. (¼ cup) flour
2 tablespoons (3T) Calvados or
  brandy

¼ pint (⅔ cup) dry (hard) cider
¼ pint (⅔ cup) chicken stock
  (bouillon)
bouquet garni
5 dessert apples, cored
2 oz. (¼ cup) butter
1 tablespoon grated lemon rind
¼ pint (⅔ cup) double (heavy)
  cream
chopped fresh parsley to garnish

Rub the chicken with salt and pepper. Heat the oil in a flameproof casserole over moderate heat. Add the chicken portions and fry for about 3-4 minutes on each side, until evenly browned. Take out the chicken and set aside.

Add the onions, celery and bacon to the casserole. Fry gently until the onions are soft but not browned. Sprinkle in the flour, stir well and cook for 1 minute. Replace the chicken and add the Calvados. Pour in the cider, stock and add the bouquet garni, stirring well. Bring to the boil. Simmer for 2 minutes.

Cut two of the apples into quarters and add to the casserole. Cover and cook in a moderately hot oven, 375°F, Gas Mark 5 for 45 minutes. Meanwhile, slice the remaining apples. Melt the butter and fry the apple slices until golden brown.

Transfer the chicken to a serving dish and strain the liquor into a saucepan. Add the lemon rind to the liquor and bring to the boil. Boil rapidly for 3-4 minutes until reduced and thickened. Taste and correct the seasoning, if necessary. Stir in the cream, reheat gently but do not allow to boil.

Pour the sauce over the chicken and garnish with the apple slices and chopped parsley.
Serves 4

Coq au Vin

2 oz. (½ cup) flour
salt
freshly ground black pepper
½ teaspoon paprika
3 lb. chicken, cut into joints
4 oz. (½ cup) butter
4 oz. shallots
6 slices streaky (fatty) bacon,
  roughly chopped
2 cloves garlic, crushed
½ teaspoon dried marjoram
½ teaspoon dried thyme
1 bay leaf

1 tablespoon finely chopped fresh
  parsley
½ pint (1¼ cups) dry red wine
½ pint (1¼ cups) chicken stock
  (bouillon)
4 oz. (1 cup) button mushrooms
4 tablespoons (⅓ cup) brandy
Garnish:
4 slices bread, crusts removed
2 oz. (¼ cup) unsalted butter,
  melted
sprigs of fresh parsley

Combine the flour, salt, pepper and paprika and coat the chicken joints well, shaking off the excess flour. Reserve this flour.

Melt 2 oz. (¼ cup) of the butter in a flameproof casserole over a gentle heat. Add the chicken joints and fry lightly for 5 minutes on each side. Add shallots, bacon and garlic. Continue to fry gently for 5 minutes, stirring occasionally, until the shallots have softened but not browned.

Sprinkle in the herbs and stir in the wine and stock. Bring to the boil. Cover and cook in a moderate oven, 350°F, Gas Mark 4 for 50 minutes.

Meanwhile, melt 1 oz. (2T) of the remaining butter and gently fry the mushrooms for 2 minutes. Pour over the brandy and ignite. Rotate the pan until the flames die down. Remove the casserole from the oven and add the mushrooms and liquor. Cover and cook for a further 10 minutes.

Melt the remaining 1 oz. (2T) butter in a saucepan over gentle heat and stir in the reserved flour. Cook the roux for 1 minute. Strain ½ pint (1¼ cups) liquor from the casserole and gradually stir into the roux. Bring to the boil, stirring constantly. Simmer for 2 minutes then pour into the casserole. Return to the oven and cook for a further 5 minutes.

To make the garnish, fry the bread slices in the butter until crisp and golden. Drain on kitchen paper then cut into triangles. Remove the casserole from the oven, taste and adjust the seasoning, if necessary. Remove the bay leaf.

Arrange the bread croûtes around the edge of the dish and garnish with parsley sprigs before serving.
Serves 4-6

Chicken in Cherry Sauce

2 oz. (¼ cup) butter
4 chicken joints
4 oz. (1 cup) onion, finely
  chopped
16 oz. can Morello cherries
chicken stock (bouillon)
1 oz. (2T) brown sugar

½ teaspoon grated nutmeg
½ teaspoon ground mace
½ teaspoon ground ginger
½ teaspoon ground cinnamon
salt
freshly ground black pepper
strips of lemon rind to garnish

Heat the butter in a frying pan over a low heat and fry the joints for
5 minutes on each side until browned. Transfer to a casserole. Gently fry
the onion in the fat remaining in the pan until soft and translucent.

Drain the cherries, reserving the juice. Make up to 1 pint (2½ cups) with
chicken stock. Add the cherry juice and stock to the pan and bring to the
boil. Stir in the cherries and remaining ingredients.

Pour over the chicken, cover the casserole and cook in a moderate
oven, 350°F, Gas Mark 4 for 1 hour or until the chicken is tender.

Transfer the joints to a serving dish and keep warm. Boil the juice to
reduce by half. Taste and adjust the seasoning, if necessary. Pour over the
chicken and garnish with the strips of lemon rind. Serve immediately.
Serves 4

Chicken in Cider

5 lb. chicken
1 pint (2½ cups) dry (hard) cider
2 oz. (¼ cup) butter
1 oz. (¼ cup) flour
1 tablespoon tomato purée
½ teaspoon dried basil
1 tablespoon chopped fresh
  parsley

salt and pepper
8 small onions
8 small, firm tomatoes
2 green peppers, cored, seeded
  and sliced

Place the chicken and cider in a large saucepan, bring to the boil and
simmer for 45 minutes. Remove the chicken and drain well, reserving the
cider. Melt the butter in a flameproof casserole and put in the chicken,
breast side down. Cook in a hot oven, 425°F, Gas Mark 7 for 20 minutes.

Meanwhile, blend the flour with a little of the reserved cider, then stir in
the remainder. Bring to the boil, stirring, and simmer for 2 minutes. Add
the tomato purée, herbs and seasoning.

Remove the chicken from the oven and place it on its back in the
casserole, so that the breast is uppermost. Pour the cider sauce over the
chicken, cover the casserole and cook in a moderate oven, 350°F, Gas
Mark 4 for 1 hour. Add the onions and cook for 30 minutes, then add the
tomatoes and pepper and continue to cook for a further 30 minutes. Taste
and adjust the seasoning, if necessary, before serving.
Serves 6-8

Devon Chicken

2 tablespoons (3T) oil
1 oz. (2T) butter
4 chicken joints
8 oz. (1½ cups) carrots, halved
8 oz. button onions
2 sticks celery, chopped
1 oz. (¼ cup) flour
¾ pint (2 cups) dry (hard) cider

2 tablespoons (3T) Worcestershire
  sauce
salt
freshly ground black pepper
1 teaspoon dry mustard
4 oz. (¾ cup) frozen peas
sprig of fresh parsley to garnish

Heat the oil and butter in a frying pan. Fry the chicken joints over a medium heat for 5 minutes on each side until golden brown. Transfer to a casserole.

Add the carrots, onions and celery to the frying pan and fry for 5 minutes, stirring occasionally, until softened and just beginning to brown. Blend in the flour and cook for 1 minute. Stir in the cider and bring to the boil, stirring constantly. Simmer for 2 minutes then add the Worcestershire sauce, salt, pepper and mustard.

Pour over the chicken, cover the casserole and cook in a moderate oven, 350°F, Gas Mark 4 for 1 hour. Add the peas and cook for a further 10-15 minutes or until the vegetables are tender.

Taste and adjust the seasoning, if necessary. Garnish with parsley before serving.

Serves 4

Paprika Chicken Casserole

3 lb. chicken
1 oz. (¼ cup) flour
½ teaspoon salt
1 tablespoon paprika
¼ teaspoon cayenne pepper
1 oz. (2T) butter or margarine
1 large onion, chopped
1 garlic clove, crushed

1 tablespoon tomato purée
2 oz. (¼ cup) button mushrooms,
  sliced
½ teaspoon dried basil
1 bay leaf
1 pint (2½ cups) chicken stock
  (bouillon)
sprigs of fresh parsley to garnish

Divide the chicken into 4 joints. Combine the flour, salt, paprika and cayenne pepper. Coat the chicken joints with the seasoned flour.

Melt the butter or margarine in a flameproof casserole over a moderate heat and fry the chicken joints for 5 minutes on each side until golden brown. Remove the chicken and add the onion and garlic to the casserole. Fry for 5 minutes until soft, but not browned.

Return the joints to the casserole and add the remaining ingredients. Bring to the boil. Cover and cook in a moderate oven, 350°F, Gas Mark 4 for 1 hour or until tender.

Taste and adjust the seasoning, if necessary. Garnish with parsley.

Serves 4

Chicken à la Mornay

Mornay sauce:
¾ pint (2 cups) milk
1 shallot, sliced
1 small carrot, sliced
½ stick celery, sliced
1 bay leaf
3 peppercorns
salt
1½ oz. (3T) butter
1½ oz. (⅓ cup) flour

3 oz. (¾ cup) Parmesan or mature
  Cheddar cheese, grated
4 chicken breasts, skinned
1 teaspoon paprika
freshly ground black pepper
2 oz. (¼ cup) butter
2 teaspoons dried marjoram
1 lb. courgettes (zucchini), sliced
1 teaspoon lemon juice
¼ pint (⅔ cup) single (light) cream

To make the sauce: place the milk, vegetables, bay leaf and seasonings in a saucepan. Bring slowly to the boil, take off the heat, cover and leave to infuse for 15 minutes.

Melt the butter in another saucepan, sprinkle in the flour and cook over a low heat for 2-3 minutes, stirring. Remove the roux from the heat. Strain the milk, discarding the flavourings. Gradually add the milk to the roux, stirring after each addition.

Return to the heat, bring to the boil, stirring constantly and simmer for 2-3 minutes until the sauce is smooth and thick. Remove from the heat and stir in two-thirds of the cheese.

Rub the chicken breasts with paprika, salt and pepper. Melt the butter in a frying pan over a moderate heat, add the chicken breasts and sprinkle with 1 teaspoon marjoram. Cook the chicken for 3-4 minutes on each side, or until evenly browned. Transfer to a casserole.

Sauté the courgettes in the butter remaining in the pan for 3 minutes, stirring occasionally. Sprinkle with the remaining marjoram, salt, pepper and lemon juice.

Arrange the courgettes around the chicken. Pour the mornay sauce over and put the lid on the casserole. Cover and cook in a moderate oven, 350°F, Gas Mark 4 for 35 minutes.

Stir in the cream and sprinkle over the remaining cheese. Cook for a further 15 minutes or until the chicken is tender. Taste and correct the seasoning. Serve immediately.

Serves 4

Greek Chicken with Tomatoes

4 chicken joints
1 lemon, juice and grated rind
¼ teaspoon ground cloves
½ teaspoon ground cinnamon
salt
freshly ground black pepper

4 tablespoons (⅓ cup) oil
6 tomatoes, peeled and chopped
2 tablespoons (3T) tomato purée
¾ pint (2 cups) chicken stock
  (bouillon)

Trim the chicken joints, removing any excess fat or skin. Mix the lemon juice, rind, cloves, cinnamon, salt and pepper together. Rub the joints with this mixture.

Heat the oil in a frying pan and gently fry the joints, turning occasionally, until they are evenly browned, about 5-7 minutes. Place in a casserole. Put the tomatoes, tomato purée and stock into the pan and stir well. Simmer for 5 minutes. Pour over the chicken, cover and cook in a moderate oven, 350°F, Gas Mark 4 for 45 minutes. Remove the lid and cook for 15 minutes.

Taste and adjust the seasoning, if necessary.

Serves 4

Braised Farmhouse Chicken

3½ lb. oven ready chicken
salt
freshly ground black pepper
6 oz. pork sausage meat
1 lemon, grated rind and juice
2 oz. (1 cup) fresh breadcrumbs
½ teaspoon dried thyme
½ teaspoon dried marjoram
½ teaspoon finely chopped fresh
  rosemary

1 egg yolk, beaten
16 button onions
2 oz. (¼ cup) butter
4 oz. (1 cup) button mushrooms,
  sliced
3 sticks celery, chopped
1 oz. (¼ cup) flour
1 pint (2½ cups) chicken stock
  (bouillon)

Season the outside and cavity of the chicken with 1 teaspoon salt and 1 teaspoon pepper. Combine the sausage meat, lemon rind and juice, breadcrumbs, herbs and seasoning. Bind the mixture with the egg yolk. Form into small balls and use these, together with half the onions, to stuff the chicken. Secure the neckskin with a small skewer.

Melt the butter in a large flameproof casserole and brown the chicken evenly on all sides. Remove. Add the remaining onions, mushrooms and celery to the casserole and sauté gently for 5 minutes, stirring occasionally. Sprinkle in the flour and stir to coat the vegetables thoroughly. Gradually pour in the stock and bring the liquid to the boil, stirring all the time.

Return the chicken to the casserole and cook, covered, in a moderate oven, 350°F, Gas Mark 4 for 1½-2 hours or until the chicken is tender. Taste and adjust the seasoning, if necessary. Serve from the casserole.

Serves 4-6

Chicken Madeira

4 tablespoons (⅓ cup) flour
salt
freshly ground black pepper
4 chicken portions
1 oz. (2T) butter
4 tablespoons (⅓ cup) oil
2 large onions, sliced
1 green pepper, cored, seeded
  and sliced
1 red pepper, cored, seeded and
  sliced

¼ teaspoon grated nutmeg
¼ teaspoon ground mace
½ pint (1¼ cups) chicken stock
  (bouillon)
1 bay leaf
8 oz. (2 cups) button mushrooms,
  sliced
2 tablespoons (3T) Madeira
¼ pint (⅔ cup) double (heavy)
  cream

Season 3 tablespoons (¼ cup) of the flour with salt and pepper. Coat the chicken portions with the seasoned flour.

Melt the butter and 2 tablespoons (3T) of the oil in a large frying pan over moderate heat. Fry the chicken portions for 3-4 minutes on each side or until golden brown. Transfer to a flameproof casserole.

Add the onions to the frying pan and fry, stirring frequently, for 3 minutes. Add the peppers and fry for a further 5 minutes, stirring occasionally, until the onions are golden brown. Place on top of the chicken. Sprinkle with nutmeg, mace, salt and pepper. Pour the stock over the chicken and vegetables and add the bay leaf. Cover the casserole and place in a moderate oven, 350°F, Gas Mark 4. Cook for 45 minutes.

Lightly sauté the mushrooms in the remaining oil for 2-3 minutes then add to the casserole. Return to the oven and cook for another 15 minutes. Transfer the chicken and vegetables to a warmed serving dish.

Blend the remaining 1 tablespoon of flour with the Madeira. Stir in the cream. Gradually pour this mixture into the casserole, stirring continuously. Bring the sauce just to boiling point, stirring constantly. Reduce the heat and cook, stirring, for 2 minutes. Taste and adjust the seasoning, if necessary. Remove the bay leaf. Pour the sauce over the chicken and vegetables and serve immediately.
Serves 4

Chicken Suprême

2 oz. (½ cup) flour
salt and pepper
½ teaspoon grated lemon rind
4 large chicken breasts
4 tablespoons (⅓ cup) oil
1 onion, finely chopped
4 oz. (1 cup) mushrooms, sliced
2 tablespoons (3T) tomato purée
1 tablespoon redcurrant jelly

¼ teaspoon powdered oregano
4 tablespoons (⅓ cup) dry
  vermouth
1 pint (2½ cups) chicken stock
  (bouillon)
2 oz. (¼ cup) tongue, cut into
  strips
2 oz. (¼ cup) ham, cut into strips
chopped fresh parsley to garnish

Mix the flour, salt, pepper and lemon rind together in a large bowl. Toss the chicken in the flour and coat well. Heat the oil in a large frying pan over moderate heat. Gently fry the chicken portions for 4 minutes on each side until lightly browned. Transfer to a casserole.

Add the onion to the pan and fry gently for 4 minutes, stirring, until soft but not browned. Add the mushrooms and cook for a further 2 minutes. Add the tomato purée, redcurrant jelly, oregano, vermouth and stock and bring to the boil, stirring. Pour over the chicken, cover the casserole and cook in a moderate oven, 350°F, Gas Mark 4 for 1 hour.

Place the chicken on a serving dish and keep warm. Boil the cooking liquor until reduced by about half. Add the tongue and ham and heat for 2 minutes. Taste and adjust the seasoning, if necessary. Pour over the chicken, sprinkle with the parsley and serve.
Serves 4

Chicken with Tarragon

3 oz. (¾ cup) flour
salt and pepper
½ teaspoon dry mustard
4 chicken joints, skinned
2 oz. (¼ cup) butter
2 shallots, finely chopped

5 tablespoons (6T) dry white wine
½ teaspoon dried tarragon
4 tablespoons (⅓ cup) chicken
  stock (bouillon)
4 tablespoons (⅓ cup) double
  (heavy) cream

Mix together the flour, salt, pepper and mustard. Coat the chicken portions evenly with the flour, shaking off any excess. Reserve excess flour.

Melt 1½ oz. (3T) of the butter in a large frying pan over moderate heat. Add the chicken joints and fry for 5-7 minutes, turning frequently, until evenly browned. Place in a casserole.

Add the shallots to the pan and fry for 5 minutes until translucent and soft, but not browned. Sprinkle in the remaining flour and mix well. Cook for 1-2 minutes but do not allow the flour to brown. Stir in the wine, tarragon and stock. Bring to the boil, stirring all the time.

Pour over chicken, cover and cook in a moderate oven, 350°F, Gas Mark 4 for 1 hour. Stir in butter and cream. Cook for 5 minutes.
Serves 4

Turkey Montgomery

2 turkey legs, each cut into 2
  portions
salt
freshly ground black pepper
4 tablespoons (⅓ cup) oil
1 onion, finely chopped
4 oz. ham (cured), cut into ½ inch
  strips
1 green pepper, cored, seeded
  and sliced

1 oz. (¼ cup) flour
½ pint (1¼ cups) chicken stock
  (bouillon)
½ pint (1¼ cups) dry (hard) cider
bouquet garni
1 tablespoon tomato purée
dash of Tabasco sauce
1 tablespoon horseradish sauce
1 tablespoon redcurrant jelly
sprig of fresh parsley to garnish

Rub the turkey portions with salt and pepper. Heat the oil in a large frying pan and fry the joints gently for 7 minutes on each side until golden brown. Transfer to a casserole.

Add the onion to the pan and fry for 5 minutes until soft but not browned. Stir in the ham and green pepper and cook slowly for 2-3 minutes. Sprinkle in the flour, then gradually stir in the stock and cider. Bring to the boil, stirring constantly. Add the bouquet garni, tomato purée and Tabasco sauce and simmer for 3 minutes.

Pour the sauce over the turkey and cook in a moderate oven, 350°F, Gas Mark 4 for 45 minutes. Stir in the horseradish sauce and redcurrant jelly and continue to cook for a further 15 minutes or until the meat is tender. Taste and adjust the seasoning, if necessary. Garnish with parsley before serving.
Serves 4

Turkey with Walnuts

1 oz. (¼ cup) flour
salt
freshly ground black pepper
1½ lb. raw turkey, sliced from the
  breast and legs
4 tablespoons (⅓ cup) oil
1 teaspoon grated lemon rind
½ teaspoon dried thyme
½ teaspoon grated nutmeg

½ pint (1¼ cups) single (light)
  cream
4 oz. (1 cup) walnut halves
2 oz. (⅓ cup) sultanas (seedless
  white raisins)
4 tablespoons (⅓ cup) port
8 oz. (2 cups) mushrooms, sliced
2 tablespoons (3T) chopped fresh
  parsley

Mix together the flour, salt and pepper. Coat the turkey with the seasoned flour. Heat the oil in a flameproof casserole over a moderate heat and fry the turkey gently, turning frequently, until just brown. Add the lemon rind, thyme and nutmeg then stir in the cream. Bring just to the boil, stirring constantly to yield a smooth sauce.

Stir in the walnuts, sultanas and port. Cover the casserole and cook in a moderate oven, 350°F, Gas Mark 4 for 45 minutes.

Stir in the mushrooms and cook for a further 30 minutes. Taste and adjust the seasoning, if necessary. Garnish with the chopped parsley. Serve with Brussels sprouts or French beans.
Serves 4

Turkey with Lemon and Capers

2 turkey breasts, split in half
  lengthwise
salt
freshly ground black pepper
4 tablespoons (⅓ cup) oil
1½ oz. (⅓ cup) flour
½ pint (1¼ cups) single (light)
  cream
¼ pint (⅔ cup) dry white wine

1 tablespoon grated lemon rind
1 teaspoon fresh or ½ teaspoon
  dried thyme
¼ teaspoon dried marjoram
2 tablespoons (3T) capers
Garnish:
few strips of thinly pared lemon
  rind
watercress

Rub the turkey with salt and pepper. Heat the oil over a moderate heat and fry the turkey gently for 4-5 minutes on each side until lightly browned. Remove and place in a casserole. Stir the flour into the pan juices then gradually stir in the cream and wine. Bring just to the boil, stirring. Lower the heat and simmer for 2 minutes.

Add the remaining ingredients and pour over the turkey. Cover the casserole and cook in a moderate oven, 350°F, Gas Mark 4 for 45 minutes or until the meat is tender.

Taste and adjust the seasoning, if necessary. Garnish with strips of lemon rind and watercress.
Serves 4

TURKEY WITH WALNUTS (Photograph: British Turkey Federation)

Goose in Grapefruit

7-8 lb. goose
salt
freshly ground black pepper
1 teaspoon ground ginger
1 teaspoon ground cloves
3 small grapefruit

2 oz. (⅓ cup) dates, chopped
2 oz. (⅓ cup) brown sugar
¼ pint (⅔ cup) grapefruit juice
¼ pint (⅔ cup) sweet white wine
2 oz. (¼ cup) butter

Split the goose down the backbone and prick the skin all over. Mix together the salt, pepper, ginger and cloves and rub over the goose. Place in a casserole and cook in a hot oven, 425°F, Gas Mark 7 for 15 minutes.

Meanwhile, thinly pare the rind from one of the grapefruit and cut into thin strips. Peel all the grapefruit, removing the pith completely. Cut two into cubes and thinly slice the remaining grapefruit.

Remove the casserole from the oven and take out the goose. Stir the chopped grapefruit, dates, sugar, grapefruit juice and wine into the casserole. Replace the goose, spooning the juices over. Cover the casserole and cook in a moderate oven, 350°F, Gas Mark 4 for 2 hours, turning and basting occasionally.

Melt the butter and add the grapefruit slices. Fry gently for 5-6 minutes, turning occasionally. Remove the goose from the oven and place on a serving dish. Strain the juices into a saucepan, squeezing the pulp to extract as much juice as possible. Boil the sauce to reduce down and thicken. Taste and correct the seasoning, if necessary. Pour the sauce over the goose and arrange the grapefruit slices on top.

Serves 6

Oriental Duck

4 tablespoons (⅓ cup) oil
4 lb. duckling, cut into 4 portions
1 chilli pepper, finely chopped
1 garlic clove, crushed
1 tablespoon tomato purée
2 tablespoons (3T) white vinegar
2 teaspoons brown sugar
salt
freshly ground black pepper

1 oz. (¼ cup) flour
½ teaspoon ground cinnamon
2 tablespoons (3T) soy sauce
¼ pint (⅔ cup) chicken stock
 (bouillon)
4 tablespoons (⅓ cup) sherry
1 green pepper, cored, seeded
 and sliced
4 oz. (1 cup) button mushrooms

Heat the oil in a large flameproof casserole over a moderate heat. Add the duck portions and fry on each side for 6-8 minutes until golden brown. Add the chilli pepper and garlic and fry for a further 2 minutes. Remove the duck and set aside.

Add the tomato purée, vinegar, sugar, salt, pepper, flour, cinnamon and soy sauce to the casserole and stir well. Gradually stir in the stock and sherry and bring to the boil. Replace the duck and spoon the sauce over the portions.

Cover and cook in a moderate oven, 350°F, Gas Mark 4 for 40 minutes. Stir in the green pepper and mushrooms and cook for a further 15 minutes. Taste and correct the seasoning.
Serves 4

Duck with Plums and Almonds

5 lb. duckling, cut into serving
 portions
salt
freshly ground black pepper
2 teaspoons ground cinnamon
½ teaspoon ground mace
2 tablespoons (3T) orange juice
2 teaspoons grated lemon rind

1 lb. plums, halved and stoned
½ pint (1¼ cups) chicken stock
 (bouillon)
2 teaspoons brown sugar
3 tablespoons (¼ cup) redcurrant
 jelly
2 oz. (½ cup) blanched almonds

Rub the duck portions with salt and pepper. Arrange in a casserole and put into a very hot oven, 450°F, Gas Mark 8 for 15 minutes until browned.

Sprinkle the cinnamon, mace and orange juice over the duck then add the lemon rind and plums. Pour in the stock and add the sugar.

Cover the casserole and cook in a moderate oven, 350°F, Gas Mark 4 for 1 hour or until the duck is tender. Skim off excess fat. Stir in the redcurrant jelly and almonds and cook for a further 5 minutes. Taste and adjust the seasoning, if necessary, before serving.
Serves 4-6

Sweet and Sour Duck with Pineapple

3 tablespoons (¼ cup) soy sauce
1 tablespoon sugar
½ teaspoon ground ginger
1 garlic clove, crushed
4 lb. duckling, cut into serving
  pieces
1 pint (2½ cups) water
1 small onion, chopped
1 bay leaf
bouquet garni
salt
freshly ground black pepper
14 oz. can pineapple chunks
2 tablespoons (3T) oil
1 tablespoon cornflour
  (cornstarch)
2 tablespoons (3T) vinegar

Combine the soy sauce, sugar, ginger and garlic in a large bowl. Add the duck pieces, toss to coat thoroughly then leave to marinate for 1 hour.

Meanwhile, place the duck giblets in a pan with the water, onion, bay leaf, bouquet garni and seasoning. Bring to the boil, skim, then cover and simmer for 1 hour. Strain, reserving the stock. Make up to 1¼ pints (3 cups) with the juice from the pineapple.

Heat the oil in a large flameproof casserole. Add the duck pieces and fry until golden brown on all sides. Pour the stock over the duck, cover the casserole and cook in a moderate oven, 350°F, Gas Mark 4 for 1 hour.

Blend the cornflour with the vinegar. Strain the liquid from the casserole and stir into the cornflour. Pour into a saucepan, bring to the boil, stirring, and cook until thickened. Add the pineapple then pour the sauce over the duck.

Return to the oven and cook uncovered for a further 10 minutes. Taste and adjust the seasoning before serving.
Serves 4

GAME CASSEROLES

Venison with Chestnuts

2 lb. lean stewing venison
Marinade:
½ pint (1 ¼ cups) red wine
1 tablespoon oil
1 tablespoon red wine vinegar
salt
6 black peppercorns, crushed
½ teaspoon allspice
6 coriander seeds, crushed
1 tablespoon chopped fresh
  rosemary

1 oz. (¼ cup) flour
freshly ground black pepper
1 teaspoon paprika
4 tablespoons (⅓ cup) oil
1 large onion, chopped
1 garlic clove, crushed
½ teaspoon grated nutmeg
1 tablespoon grated orange rind
½ pint (1 ¼ cups) beef stock
  (bouillon)
1 lb. chestnuts, peeled
1 tablespoon brown sugar

Trim any excess fat from the venison and cut the meat into 1 inch cubes. Combine all the ingredients for the marinade and stir well. Add the venison, cover the dish and leave to marinate for 24 hours, basting occasionally.

With a slotted spoon, remove the meat from the marinade and wipe dry. Strain and reserve the marinade. Mix the flour with salt, pepper and paprika and use to coat the venison. Heat the oil in a frying pan and fry the meat, turning occasionally, for 8 minutes until evenly browned. Transfer to a casserole.

Add the onion and garlic to the oil remaining in the pan and fry for 6-7 minutes until just beginning to brown. Stir in the reserved marinade, nutmeg, orange rind and stock. Bring to the boil and pour over the meat. Cover and place in a moderate oven, 350°F, Gas Mark 4. Cook for 1 hour.

Stir in the chestnuts and the sugar and cook for a further 45 minutes. Remove the lid and cook for a further 15 minutes or until the meat is tender. Taste and adjust the seasoning, if necessary.
Serves 6

Rabbit in Mustard

4 lb. rabbit, cut into serving pieces
Marinade:
½ pint (1 ¼ cups) light ale
1 garlic clove, crushed
salt
freshly ground black pepper
1 teaspoon chopped fresh sage

3 tablespoons (¼ cup) oil
6 slices streaky (fatty) bacon,
  derinded and chopped

1 large onion, diced
1 teaspoon chopped fresh thyme
1 teaspoon chopped fresh
  rosemary
1 tablespoon French mustard
1 tablespoon cornflour
  (cornstarch)
¼ pint (⅔ cup) single (light) cream
sprigs of fresh parsley to garnish

Place the rabbit in a casserole and add the marinade ingredients. Leave for 12 hours at room temperature, basting occasionally. Remove the joints and dry well. Reserve the marinade.

Heat the oil in a flameproof casserole and add the bacon and onion. Fry gently for 5 minutes until the onion is soft but not browned. Remove the onion and bacon with a slotted spoon. Add the rabbit joints to the casserole and cook for 8-10 minutes, turning occasionally, until they are evenly browned.

Return the bacon and onion to the casserole, pour the marinade over and add the herbs, mustard and seasoning. Bring to the boil. Cover and cook in a moderate oven, 350°F, Gas Mark 4 for 1-1 ¼ hours until the meat is tender.

Transfer the rabbit to a warmed serving dish. Blend the cornflour with 2 tablespoons (3T) of the cooking liquor. Place casserole over a low heat and gradually stir in the cornflour. Bring to the boil, stirring. Simmer for 2 minutes. Lower the heat and stir in the cream. Heat gently without boiling.

Taste and adjust the seasoning, if necessary. Pour the sauce over the rabbit, garnish with the parsley sprigs and serve.
Serves 4

Hare in Madeira Sauce

1 young hare, cut into 4 joints
½ oz. (2T) flour
1 teaspoon chopped fresh or ⅓
  teaspoon dried sage
3 oz. (⅓ cup) butter
4 oz. (1 cup) button mushrooms

⅓ pint (1 cup) Madeira
½ teaspoon chopped fresh herbs
salt
freshly ground black pepper
chopped fresh parsley to garnish

Sprinkle the hare with the flour and sage. Melt 2 oz. (¼ cup) of the butter in a large frying pan and fry the hare, stirring occasionally, until evenly browned. Transfer to a casserole.

Melt the remaining butter in the pan, add the mushrooms and sauté gently for 1-2 minutes. Add to the casserole with the Madeira, herbs and seasoning. Cover the casserole and cook in a moderately hot oven, 375°F, Gas Mark 5 for 1 hour.

Garnish with chopped parsley before serving.
Serves 4

Chiltern Pigeons

4 young pigeons
salt
freshly ground black pepper
3 tablespoons (¼ cup) oil
1 onion, finely diced
1 oz. (¼ cup) flour
4 oz. (¾ cup) dried apricots,
  soaked overnight and drained
8 cloves

1-2 tablespoons curry powder
1 tablespoon concentrated orange
  juice
¼ teaspoon cayenne pepper
½ teaspoon ground allspice
½ teaspoon ground cinnamon
1 tablespoon brown sugar
1 pint (2½ cups) chicken stock
  (bouillon)

Wash the pigeons, discarding the giblets. Dry thoroughly and season with salt and pepper. Heat the oil in a large flameproof casserole and fry the pigeons, two at a time, turning frequently, for 10 minutes until evenly browned. Remove.

Add the onion to the casserole and fry for about 5 minutes, stirring occasionally, until soft but not browned. Stir in the flour, apricots, cloves, curry powder, orange juice, cayenne, allspice, cinnamon and sugar.

Gradually stir in the stock and bring to the boil, stirring. Simmer for 2 minutes. Return the pigeons to the casserole, cover and cook in a moderate oven, 350°F, Gas Mark 4 for 1-1¼ hours or until the pigeons are tender.

Transfer the pigeons to a warmed serving dish and boil the sauce for 1-2 minutes to reduce slightly and thicken. Taste and adjust the seasoning, if necessary. Pour the sauce over the pigeons and serve.
Serves 4

SUPPER CASSEROLES

Virginian Supper

6 oz. egg noodles
salt
12 oz. can condensed mushroom
  soup
¼ pint (⅔ cup) milk
4 oz. (1 cup) cheese, grated
2 oz. (½ cup) onion, chopped

1 lb. cooked ham (cured), cut into
  1 inch cubes
3 oz. fresh or frozen peas
freshly ground black pepper
1 teaspoon English mustard
2 teaspoons paprika

Cook the noodles in boiling salted water for 10 minutes or until just tender. Drain thoroughly and place in a casserole.

Blend the soup with the milk then add to the noodles. Stir in the remaining ingredients and place in a moderate oven, 350°F, Gas Mark 4. Cook for 30-40 minutes or until thick, creamy and lightly browned.

Taste and adjust the seasoning, if necessary, before serving.
Serves 4

Bacon and Bean Supper

1½ lb. bacon collar joint (smoked
  picnic shoulder of pork)
1½ oz. (3T) butter
8 oz. leeks, washed trimmed and
  sliced
1 small onion, chopped
2 tablespoons (3T) flour
salt
freshly ground black pepper
1 teaspoon English mustard

½ teaspoon dried marjoram
¾ pint (2 cups) light stock
  (bouillon)
4 oz. (¾ cup) carrots, peeled and
  sliced
7½ oz. can red kidney beans,
  drained
1 tablespoon chopped fresh
  parsley

Remove the rind and excess fat from the bacon. Cut the meat into 3 inch cubes. Place in a pan of cold water and bring slowly to the boil. Drain thoroughly.

Melt the butter in a pan over a moderate heat. Add the leeks and onion and fry gently for 5 minutes until soft but not browned. Stir in the flour, salt, pepper, mustard and marjoram, then gradually stir in the stock. Bring to the boil, stirring, and cook for 1 minute to give a smooth sauce.

Place the bacon and carrots in a casserole and pour the sauce over. Cover and cook in a moderate oven, 350°F, Gas Mark 4 for 45 minutes. Add the kidney beans and continue cooking for a further 15 minutes. Taste and adjust the seasoning if necessary. Sprinkle with the chopped parsley.
Serves 4

Devilled Gammon

3 tablespoons (¼ cup) oil
4 gammon steaks (smoked ham
  slices)
1 green pepper, cored, seeded
  and sliced
Sauce:
1 tablespoon chilli sauce
2 tablespoons (3T) lemon juice

1 small onion, finely chopped
2 teaspoons English mustard
1 tablespoon Worcestershire
  sauce
salt and pepper
5 tablespoons (6T) lime juice
1½ tablespoons (2T) brown sugar

Heat the oil in a flameproof casserole over a moderate heat. Add the gammon steaks, two at a time, and cook for 4-5 minutes on each side until lightly browned. Return the other two steaks to the casserole and add the green pepper.

Combine all the sauce ingredients. Mix thoroughly then pour over the meat. Cover the casserole and place in a moderate oven, 325°F, Gas Mark 3. Cook for 1 hour, basting occasionally, or until the meat is tender. Taste and adjust the seasoning, if necessary before serving.
Serves 4

Kidney Supper

12 lambs' kidneys
3 oz. (¾ cup) flour
salt
freshly ground black pepper
½ teaspoon paprika
1 teaspoon grated lemon rind
8 slices streaky (fatty) bacon,
  derinded and chopped

2 oz. (¼ cup) butter
2 onions, sliced
1 green pepper, cored, seeded
  and sliced
1 tablespoon soy sauce
½ pint (1¼ cups) hot beef stock
  (bouillon)

Wash, skin and core the kidneys. Mix the flour with salt, pepper, paprika and lemon rind. Coat the kidneys evenly with the flour mixture, shaking off any excess. Coat the bacon in the excess flour.

Melt the butter in a frying pan over a gentle heat, add the kidneys and fry, turning frequently, until evenly browned. Transfer to a casserole. Add the bacon, onions and green pepper to the pan and fry gently for 5 minutes, stirring frequently. Stir in the soy sauce, then pour in the stock gradually, stirring, to give a smooth sauce. Bring to the boil then pour over the kidneys.

Cover the casserole and cook in a moderate oven, 350°F, Gas Mark 4 for 35-40 minutes, or until the kidneys are cooked and tender. Taste and adjust the seasoning, if necessary.
Serves 3-4

Hungarian Supper

8 oz. frankfurters, cut into 2 inch
  pieces
8 oz. Hungarian salami, chopped
1 tablespoon soy sauce
2 tablespoons (3T) lemon juice
3 tablespoons (¼ cup) oil
2 onions, sliced
8 oz. (2 cups) button mushrooms,
  sliced
2 apples, peeled, cored and diced
1 tablespoon flour

salt
freshly ground black pepper
½ teaspoon paprika
1½ teaspoons caraway seeds,
  crushed
½ pint (1¼ cups) medium (hard)
  cider
10 oz. carrots, cooked
8 oz. green noodles
1 oz. (2T) butter

Put the frankfurters and salami into a bowl. Add the soy sauce and lemon juice and leave to marinate for 2 hours, basting occasionally. Drain the meat, reserving the marinade.

Heat the oil and gently fry the onions for 5 minutes until soft but not browned. Add the mushrooms and apples and sauté for 2 minutes. Stir in the flour, salt, pepper, paprika and caraway seeds. Gradually pour in the cider, stirring all the time and bring to the boil. Simmer for 2 minutes. Stir in the marinade.

Place the frankfurters and salami in a shallow casserole and pour the sauce over. Cover and cook in a moderate oven, 350°F, Gas Mark 4 for 35 minutes. Remove the lid, stir in the carrots and return to the oven for 5-10 minutes.

Meanwhile, cook the noodles in boiling salted water for 10 minutes, or until just tender. Drain and arrange around the edge of a serving dish. Dot with the butter.

Remove the casserole from the oven. Taste and adjust the seasoning, if necessary. Pile into the centre of the noodles.

Serves 4

HUNGARIAN SUPPER (Photograph: Mattessons)

FISH CASSEROLES

Cod Provençal

4 × 6 oz. cod steaks
salt
freshly ground black pepper
juice of ½ lemon
3 tablespoons (¼ cup) oil
2 onions, finely chopped
2 lb. tomatoes, skinned and
  chopped
1 garlic clove, crushed
1 green pepper, cored, seeded
  and sliced

½ teaspoon dried chervil
½ teaspoon dried tarragon
½ teaspoon French mustard
2 tablespoons (3T) tomato purée
1½ tablespoons (2T) capers
¼ pint (⅔ cup) dry red wine or fish
  stock (bouillon)
Garnish:
½ lemon, sliced
sprigs of fresh parsley

Season the cod steaks with salt and pepper. Sprinkle with lemon juice.

Heat the oil in a frying pan over a moderate heat. Fry the steaks for 2-3 minutes on each side. Remove. Add the onions, tomatoes, garlic and green pepper to the pan and fry for 4 minutes, stirring frequently. Add the remaining ingredients and bring to the boil.

Place the cod in a buttered casserole and pour the sauce over. Cover and cook in a moderate oven, 350°F, Gas Mark 4, for 35-40 minutes until the fish is tender.

Place the fish on a serving dish. Heat the sauce in a pan to boiling then boil for 2-3 minutes until reduced and thickened. Taste and adjust the seasoning if necessary. Pour the sauce over the fish and garnish with lemon slices and parsley.
Serves 4

Kipper and Potato Casserole

1 lb. potatoes, peeled and diced
1 onion, grated
2 teaspoons flour
salt
freshly ground black pepper
¼ teaspoon dried dill

½ teaspoon dry mustard
¼ pint (⅔ cup) water
4 kipper fillets
1½ oz. (3T) butter
¼ pint (⅔ cup) soured cream

Parboil the potatoes in boiling water for 5 minutes. Drain. Mix the potatoes with the onion and place in the bottom of a shallow casserole.

Combine the flour, salt, pepper, dill and mustard. Blend to a smooth paste with a little water, then stir in remaining water. Pour over vegetables.

Roll up the kipper fillets and lay on top of the vegetables. Dot with the butter. Cover and cook in a moderate oven, 350°F, Gas Mark 4 for 50 minutes. Stir in the soured cream and cook, covered, for a further 10 minutes. Serve with baked tomatoes.
Serves 4

Seafood Chowder

3 oz. streaky (fatty) bacon
1 oz. (2T) butter
1 onion, chopped
4 potatoes, peeled and chopped
1½ oz. (⅓ cup) flour
¾ pint (2 cups) fish stock
  (bouillon)
salt
freshly ground black pepper
blade of mace (optional)
1 bay leaf
¼ teaspoon cayenne pepper
½ teaspoon dried marjoram

1½ lb. mixed white fish (cod,
  haddock, halibut, hake)
4 oz. (¾ cup) shelled mussels
4 oz. (¾ cup) peeled prawns
  (shrimp)
¼ pint (⅔ cup) double (heavy)
  cream
Garnish:
1 tablespoon chopped fresh
  chives
1 tablespoon chopped fresh
  parsley

Heat the bacon in a large flameproof casserole over a moderate heat for 6-8 minutes or until the fat is beginning to run. Add the butter. When the butter has melted, stir in the onion and potatoes and place in a moderately hot oven, 375°F, Gas Mark 5 for 15 minutes until browned.

Sprinkle in the flour and cook, stirring, for 1 minute. Gradually stir in the stock. Add the salt, pepper, mace, bay leaf, cayenne and marjoram and bring to the boil. Cut the white fish into 2 inch pieces. Add to the casserole, cover and cook in a moderate oven, 350°F, Gas Mark 4 for 30 minutes.

Stir in the mussels and prawns and cook on top of the cooker, uncovered, for 15 minutes. Remove from the heat and gradually stir in the cream. Taste and correct the seasoning, if necessary.

Garnish with the chives and parsley and serve.
Serves 4-6

VEGETABLE AND FRUIT CASSEROLES

Ratatouille

2 aubergines (eggplants) trimmed
 and cut into ¼ inch slices
salt
4 tablespoons (⅓ cup) oil
1 large onion, sliced
1 garlic clove, finely chopped
1 green pepper, cored, seeded
 and sliced
1 red pepper, cored, seeded and
 sliced

4 courgettes (zucchini), trimmed
 and cut into ½ inch slices
2 tablespoons (3T) chopped fresh
 parsley
1 teaspoon chopped fresh or ⅓
 teaspoon dried basil
½ teaspoon chopped fresh or ¼
 teaspoon dried marjoram
freshly ground black pepper
6 tomatoes, peeled and chopped

Sprinkle the aubergine slices with salt and leave to drain for 30 minutes. Rinse and dry thoroughly.

Heat the oil in a flameproof casserole, add the onion and garlic and fry gently for 5 minutes until soft but not browned. Add the aubergine slices and fry for 2 minutes on each side, adding a little more oil if necessary.

Add the peppers and courgettes and fry for 2 minutes. Sprinkle in the herbs and seasoning. Add the tomatoes. Cover the casserole and cook in a moderate oven, 325°F, Gas Mark 3 for 35-45 minutes. Remove the lid and cook for a further 15 minutes. Serve either hot or cold.
Serves 4

Braised Red Cabbage

2 oz. (¼ cup) butter
1 small red cabbage, shredded
¼ teaspoon mixed spice
salt
freshly ground black pepper

2 tablespoons (3T) cider
4 cooking apples, peeled, cored
 and sliced
1 tablespoon honey
2 oz. (½ cup) walnut halves

Grease a medium casserole generously with the butter. Add the cabbage. Mix together the spice, salt, black pepper and cider and pour over the cabbage. Cover the casserole and cook in a moderate oven, 325°F, Gas Mark 3 for 1¼ hours.

Add the apples, honey and walnuts and mix well. Recover the casserole and continue to cook for 30-40 minutes, tossing occasionally, until tender.
Serves 4

RATATOUILLE *(Photograph: Carmel Produce Information Bureau)*

Vegetable Medley

3 tablespoons (¼ cup) oil
  (approximately)
1 onion, chopped
2 sticks celery, trimmed and
  chopped
2 lb. potatoes, peeled and sliced
8 oz. carrots, peeled and sliced
8 oz. leeks, trimmed, washed and
  sliced
4 slices streaky (fatty) bacon,
  derinded and chopped

15 oz. can tomatoes
¼ pint (⅔ cup) beef stock
  (bouillon)
salt
freshly ground black pepper
2 teaspoons paprika
1 teaspoon dry mustard
¼ teaspoon dried basil
¼ teaspoon dried marjoram
1 tablespoon brown sugar
chopped fresh parsley to garnish

Heat the oil in a large frying pan over a moderate heat. Add the onion and celery and fry, stirring occasionally, for 3-4 minutes until the onion is soft but not brown. Remove the onion and celery with a slotted spoon.

Add the potatoes to the pan and fry, stirring occasionally, for 6-8 minutes until golden brown. Add more oil if necessary. Remove the potatoes. Fry the carrots and leeks for 3-4 minutes then remove.

Return the onion and celery to the pan and add all the remaining ingredients, but not the potatoes, carrots or leeks. Bring to the boil and simmer for 2 minutes.

Arrange layers of potatoes, carrots and leeks in a casserole. Pour the tomato mixture over the top. Cover and cook in a moderate oven, 350°F, Gas Mark 4 for 45 minutes until the vegetables are tender. Taste and correct the seasoning. Sprinkle with the chopped parsley to garnish.
Serves 4

Glazed Onions

1 lb. onions, sliced
3 oz. (¼ cup) walnut halves
1 oz. (2T) butter
2 tablespoons (3T) clear honey
1 tablespoon chilli sauce
¼ pint (⅔ cup) chicken stock
  (bouillon)

salt
freshly ground black pepper
¼ teaspoon mixed spice
few drops of Worcestershire sauce
chopped fresh parsley to garnish

Place the onions in the base of a greased shallow ovenproof dish. Scatter with the nuts. Combine the remaining ingredients and pour over the onions and nuts.

Cover the dish and cook in a moderate oven, 325°F, Gas Mark 3 for 1¼ hours, or until the onions are tender and well browned. Toss the mixture occasionally during cooking.

Garnish with chopped parsley before serving.
Serves 4

Spiced Carrots

1 ½ lb. carrots, peeled and cut into
  1 inch slices
3 shallots, sliced
2 oz. (¼ cup) butter
2 oz. (⅓ cup) sultanas (seedless
  white raisins)
2 oz. (½ cup) flaked almonds

salt
freshly ground black pepper
½ teaspoon ground cinnamon
½ teaspoon cumin seeds
1 teaspoon dried thyme
1 tablespoon brown sugar
chopped fresh parsley to garnish

Toss the carrots and shallots together. Melt the butter in a shallow flameproof casserole and add the vegetables. Fry gently for 3-4 minutes, turning frequently. Add the remaining ingredients and pour over just enough water to cover.

Put the lid on the casserole and place in a moderate oven, 350°F, Gas Mark 4. Cook for 45 minutes or until the carrots are tender. Taste and adjust the seasoning if necessary.

Sprinkle with chopped parsley before serving.
Serves 4

Braised Celery

3 heads of celery
½ oz. (1 T) dripping or lard
  (shortening)
2 slices bacon, derinded and
  chopped
2 carrots, peeled and diced
2 onions, diced
2 oz. (½ cup) mushrooms,
  chopped

2 tomatoes, peeled and chopped
bouquet garni
salt
freshly ground black pepper
½ pint (1 ¼ cups) chicken or herb
  stock (bouillon)

Trim the celery, removing any damaged stalks and leaves. Separate the stalks, scrub clean in cold water and cut into 5 inch pieces. Arrange in a shallow casserole.

Melt the fat in a pan over a moderate heat and fry the bacon for 2-3 minutes. Add the remaining vegetables and fry gently, stirring until lightly browned. Add the bouquet garni, salt and pepper and pour in the stock, stirring well.

Pour over the celery, cover the casserole and cook in a moderate oven, 350°F, Gas Mark 4 for 1½-1¾ hours or until the celery is tender.

Transfer the celery to a serving dish and keep warm. Strain the liquor into a saucepan and boil rapidly to reduce to a glaze. Pour over the celery and serve.
Serves 6

Chick Pea Casserole

8 oz. (1⅓ cups) chick peas, soaked
  overnight
salt
1 garlic clove, crushed
1 onion, chopped
1 lb. tomatoes, skinned, seeded
  and chopped
8 oz. (3 cups) cabbage, shredded

½ green pepper, cored, seeded
  and chopped
2 tablespoons (3T) oil
1 teaspoon ground ginger
pinch of ground cloves
freshly ground black pepper
¼ pint (⅔ cup) stock (bouillon)

Drain the chick peas and place in a saucepan. Pour over sufficient water to cover and add ½ teaspoon salt. Simmer for 1½ hours or until tender.

Meanwhile fry the garlic and vegetables in the oil until soft but not brown. Stir in the ginger, cloves, salt and pepper. Transfer the mixture to a greased casserole. Drain the chick peas and add to the casserole. Pour the stock over.

Cover and cook in a moderate oven 350°F, Gas Mark 4 for 20-30 minutes.
Serves 4-6

Mixed Fruit Compote

6 oz. (1 cup) dried apricots,
  soaked overnight
6 oz. (1 cup) prunes, soaked
  overnight
3 oz. (½ cup) sultanas (seedless
  white raisins)
2 oz. (⅓ cup) dates, roughly
  chopped
1 cooking apple, peeled and
  quartered

1 orange, peeled and sliced
1 lemon, juice and grated rind
3 tablespoons (¼ cup) honey
½ teaspoon ground cinnamon
½ teaspoon ground ginger
6 cloves
2 oz. (¼ cup) flaked almonds

Drain the apricots and prunes. Arrange all the fruit in a shallow casserole dish. Sprinkle the lemon juice and rind over the fruit.

Combine the honey, cinnamon, ginger and cloves, then stir in 4 tablespoons (⅓ cup) water. Pour over the fruit and sprinkle with the nuts.

Cover and cook in a moderate oven, 350°F, Gas Mark 4 for 30-35 minutes. Remove the lid and continue cooking for another 15 minutes until the liquid is syrupy and the fruit is tender. Serve immediately with fresh whipped cream.
Serves 4

Pears in Red Wine

½ pint (1¼ cups) red wine
4 tablespoons (⅓ cup) water
3 oz. (¼ cup + 2T) sugar
2 cinnamon sticks or ½ teaspoon
  ground cinnamon

3 tablespoons (¼ cup) redcurrant
  jelly
6 cloves
6 firm ripe dessert pears

Place the wine, water, sugar, cinnamon, redcurrant jelly and cloves in a
flameproof casserole. Heat gently until the sugar and jelly have dissolved.

Peel the pears and add to the casserole. Spoon the syrup over the pears.
Cover and cook in a moderate oven, 325°F, Gas Mark 3 for 20-30 minutes
or until the fruit is tender.

Transfer the pears to a serving dish. Boil the cooking liquid rapidly until
reduced slightly and thickened. Pour over the fruit. Chill before serving
with cream.
Serves 6

Bananas in Orange

6 bananas, peeled
2 teaspoons cornflour (cornstarch)
¼ pint (⅔ cup) fresh orange juice
grated rind of 1 orange

2 oz. (¾ cup) desiccated
  (shredded) coconut
2 tablespoons (3T) brown sugar
1 oz. (2T) butter

Cut the bananas in half lengthwise, then into quarters. Place in a greased
baking dish.

Blend the cornflour with a little of the orange juice until smooth then stir
in the remainder. Pour over the fruit. Mix the orange rind, coconut and
sugar together and sprinkle evenly over the bananas.

Dot with the butter and cook in a moderate oven, 350°F, Gas Mark 4 for
45 minutes until the fruit is tender and the sauce is syrupy. Serve
immediately.
Serves 4

INDEX

INDEX

PDO 80-193